THE FLY-FISHING PREDATOR

The Fly-Fishing

Predator

RAYMOND C. SHEWNACK

UNIVERSITY OF NEW MEXICO PRESS

ALBUQUERQUE

Printed in China

14 13 12 11 10 09   1 2 3 4 5 6

Library of Congress Cataloging-in-Publication Data

Shewnack, Raymond C., 1949–
The fly-fishing predator / Raymond C. Shewnack.
            p. cm.
ISBN 978-0-8263-4626-1 (pbk. : alk. paper)
1. Fly fishing. I. Title.
SH456.S523 2009
799.12'4—dc22

                        2008034990

Designed and typeset by Mina Yamashita.
Composed in Minion Pro, an Adobe Original typeface designed
by Robert Slimbach. Display composed in Frutiger 77
Black Condensed, designed by Adrian Frutiger in 1976.

THIRTY-SOME YEARS AGO, a friend asked me if I wanted to go fly-fishing with him. I had fished with bait and lures most of my young life, but with minimum knowledge and passion. I had a vague inkling of what he was offering, but, being an adventurous sort, I accepted.

My friend was already an accomplished fly angler at the age of twenty-two, so he assisted me in my flailing efforts. Shortly after experiencing the challenges and rewards of fishing with a fly, he introduced me to fly tying.

This was the era before barbless hooks, so fly-fishing embedded itself deep and solid into my soul and psyche. Because we had other common interests . . . mostly girls and golf . . . we became better friends and, eventually, roommates.

Over the years, our lives have wandered in opposite directions, but we have always kept in touch and occasionally fished together. Even though some of our trips may have been separated by a number of years, we never miss a hitch and take up right where we last left off when we are fishing together.

There is not a fishing day that goes by when I do not thank Peter Syme for introducing me to this enchanting pastime.

I can never repay him, but I hope that in some small way, through this dedication, he understands how much I value that first day, and all the days that followed, and all the days still to come.

He exposed me to my own predator instincts. ▪

Contents

Acknowledgements

Teamwork is the essence of life. No book can be completed without teamwork. I am grateful to many people, some named and some unnamed but just as valuable, for their contributions to this book.

Thank you to all the anglers with whom I have had the pleasure of sharing a stream and streamside chats. I am especially thankful for Bill Frangos, my partner in our first book, *49 Trout Streams of New Mexico*, who provided the vast majority of photos included in this project.

Thank you to Vicki Kerr-Wemple, wildlife illustrator and graphic designer, who lovingly and meticulously provided the impeccable illustrations that launch each chapter. She is a longtime friend, and I have always admired her artistic skill and her fine character.

Thank you to Jim Belshaw, who continues to be a good friend and copy editor extraordinaire.

Thank you to Luther Wilson and the entire team at the University of New Mexico Press for their professional assistance.

And, most of all, a sincere and loving thanks to my wife, Ann, who understands my obsession with fly-fishing and who still encourages me to pick up my gear and go fishing.

Introduction

Watch

A red-tailed hawk soars fifty feet above the sage and chamisa-dotted plain, his keen eyes alert for a movement that will reveal his next meal. He sees it at the base of a small bush. He adjusts his flight feathers at the wing tips then pressures his tail feathers to shift his flight pattern. He begins a slow turn.

A cottontail scratches the ground near the bush. She munches tender blades of grama grass, twitching her nose, scanning all directions, sensitive to a sign of danger.

The raptor circles back so his shadow from the setting sun fades behind him. He drops to ten feet over the prairie, gliding silently toward his prey.

Oblivious to the danger above, the rabbit hops from the shadows to reach a new tuft of succulent grass. Suddenly, she sees a dark shape over her shoulder, but it is too late. The hawk grabs her and lifts her from the ground.

Listen

A gray fox moves carefully along the snow-covered bank of a rivulet. He stops, cocks his head, and listens for the telltale sound of mouse movement under the snow. He discerns a subtle shuffling and focuses his attention to determine the exact location.

Standing statue-like, the fox tenses in preparation for the pounce. He springs into the air and lands with all four paws and his snout on the point of attack. The snow compresses under his weight and he feels movement, and he closes his jaws on the rodent.

Sense

Lying in wait at the base of a juniper tree, the bobcat catches the scent of a chipmunk. The rodent is scratching in the fallen needles in search of berries. The cat's legs twitch as she establishes her grip on the soil, so when she lunges, the action will be swift and sure. The chipmunk moves a foot closer and squats to gnaw on his latest morsel.

The cat springs from the shadows and scoops up her meal.

These predators live by a common rule. They must capture their sustenance and expend less energy in the effort than they gain from the bounty. That is the law of survival.

Early man needed the skills and instincts of a predator to survive. He required keen eyesight, sensitive hearing, and an acute sense of smell in order to endure.

We are fortunate today that our survival is no longer dependent on our hunting prowess. However, you can hone your hunting skills, sharpen your senses, and shift your perspective to pursue the joy and success of Predator Fly-Fishing.

This book is about improving your fly-fishing experience. Fly-fishing victory can be measured in a variety of ways. You might equate it to the number of fish you catch, or to the size of the fish you land, or to simply catching the most challenging fish in the water. Your definition will fit your personality. In the following chapters, you will discover how to transform your pursuit from that of an angler to a fly-fishing predator.

Chapter 1 is about the tools of the trade you will need to gain the predator advantage.

Until recently in human history, humankind depended solely on his own hands, teeth, and strength for his food and safety. There came a time when his emerging intelligence suggested he could use tools other than those with which nature had equipped him. He discovered he could strike a heavier blow to his enemy with a broken branch than his unaided fist. He learned he could crack nuts and shellfish more easily with a stone than his own back teeth. He delighted to find that a hurled rock could bring down small animals that had scurried beyond his reach. These observations marked a great step in advancing his struggle to master his environment. He had become a tool user.

At first, after learning these lessons, primitive man merely used sticks and stones that were handy, discarding them the moment their need was over. Then, through experience, he discovered that certain forms of tools were more useful than others and deemed them worth keeping and carrying about. He found they could be still further improved with a little trimming and shaping. A club was easier to wield if twigs and irregular projections were removed. When he scraped a straight, slender branch down to a point, it made an effective dart. A few chips knocked off the side of a flint rock gave it a rough edge that could be used to cut instead of tear raw meat. With these lessons, he had become not merely a tool user, but a tool maker.

Modern fly-fishing tools are superior implements that make your angling easier and more efficient. These are the tools to use in your transformation.

The middle chapters are about sharpening your fly-fishing skills, from learning how to read the water to mastering the hooking and landing technique.

Imagine you are hiking through the forest and you come upon a man working feverishly to saw down a tree.

"What are you doing?" you ask.

"It's obvious!" he answers between strokes and deep breaths. "I'm sawing down this tree."

"You look exhausted, and you are drenched with sweat!" you reply. "How long have you been at it?"

"Over six hours," he says after wiping his brow with the back of his sleeve. "I'm beat! This is hard work."

"Why don't you take a break and sharpen your saw?" you ask. "I am absolutely certain it will go easier and faster."

"I don't have time to sharpen the saw," he says emphatically. "I'm too busy sawing!"

This analogy is not new or original, but it does serve as an example you can follow to improve your odds of success. Spend a little time sharpening the skills that can make you a better angler, and then put into practice the skills you learn so that every time you are on the water, you will be more effective and productive.

Conclusion

In the final chapter, you will see how all of these components fit together to improve your success. And then you, too, can reap the rewards of a Fly-Fishing Predator. ∎

Gain the Predator Advantage

Comparing a wolf pack stalking a herd of bison to an angler pursuing a rising trout may seem unconventional. But watch the angler apply what he has learned to catch the fish. Watch a wolf pack work together in the hunt. Each has developed predator skills.

The sun sets, daylight dims to dusk, and the wolf pack's alpha male picks up the scent of bison. The pack follows his lead. They crest the hill and hunker down in the filtered shadows under a pine stand. Below them, in a narrow draw, a herd of bison grazes. The wolves approach with care and skill then burst into a full run, surrounding the unsuspecting bison. After a brief chase and struggle, a weak, old bull succumbs to the pack. Wolves are social animals. They work in teams to capture their prey. Older animals teach the younger, less experienced members of the pack how to be more efficient predators. Just as young wolves depend on their elders for education, so too do anglers depend on experienced mentors and technology to develop and deliver tools to make their pursuits more productive, more efficient, and more enjoyable.

Fly-fishing tools have transformed anglers from the users of fundamental equipment like spears and handlines to the owners of an incredible array of apparatuses. Each item is the result of anglers saying, "There has got to be a better way." Some devices are necessary and some are peripheral.

Tools give you a predator advantage.

When you first step into a river, there may be a lot of fish within twenty feet of you. As the water swirls around rocks and tree stumps, you can visualize likely holding spots, where you will find concentrations of fish. With effort and dexterity, you can present a fly to these targets with a handline, but it takes a tremendous amount of skill and luck to fling the fly, control the line on the water, recognize the take, strike at the appropriate time, and then land the fish.

Tools alter the angler's potential. They bring fifty feet within your range. With the appropriate tools, you can control your line around obstacles. You can feel the moment the fish takes the fly. You can have leverage and shock-absorbing capability to land the fish easily.

You have an endless selection of tools, toys, and trinkets to use. The predator's primary instruments are the fly rod and reel, the fly line, the leader, and then the fly of choice. These tools impact the degree of efficiency you can attain. Two other items that do not fit the "need" category, but are beneficial to the hunt, are your waders and tackle pack.

Each device contributes to your predator strategy and will aid in your success.

The fly rod is like the landscape painter's brush. It is the extension of oneself. A landscape artist begins with a blank canvas. He first lays down background colors, and then the image emerges layer by layer. Each brushstroke contributes to the complete picture. With each stroke of the rod, the angler adds to the complete image of the angling day. The fly rod is the main tool used at every moment of the hunt, and in every stroke of the painting.

Mechanically, the fly rod is a lever that gives you the ability to transfer power from your arm, wrist, and hand and impart it to the fly line. This energy then moves down the line, losing intensity with every yard. But when a cast is performed well, it still has the oomph to extend a fly fifty feet and lay that fly gently onto the water's surface. Without this tool, you can only dangle a fly about fifteen feet away. (The good news is that to be a productive fly-fishing predator, you are not required to cast fifty feet.) The fly rod gives you the advantage of reaching many more prey without revealing your presence.

The rod is the first link in the connection between angler and fish. It begins the process of delivering the fly to all the places you should fish. How to pick those places is covered in chapter 3. The fly rod is the tool that improves your ability to be a predator.

With the aid of the rod and line, the author can reach every part of this hole without moving position.

It makes you faster and stronger than you otherwise would be. It lets you reach far-ther. It improves your stealth by keeping your shadow and profile out of the prey's win-dow. It assists you in controlling the direction of the cast and aids in management of drag. These subjects are covered in detail in later chapters.

Fly rods give you predator advantage!

The physical attributes of the tool are what give you the advantage. There are a multitude of discussions and arguments about what length, weight, and materials make for the best fly rod. Depending on fishing conditions, one rod may work slightly better than another. The fly rod is the most critical predator tool in the hunt, and what you use should be based on personal preference. Whether you choose the tradition of bamboo or the class of contemporary graphite, a 2-weight or a 7-weight, a long rod or a short one, it is your decision.

When it comes to the fly rod, the fly-fishing predator will use this tool to capture more prey than he can without it. How to use this valuable tool to increase your predator advantage is covered in chapter 2.

One afternoon not long ago, my friend John and I were fishing side by side up a little mountain stream in the Colorado Rockies. As the watercourse curved back and forth,

The line forms a tight loop when the author casts into a nice run.

the better holding areas alternately presented better opportunities to each of us. After about three hours of successful fishing, John's reel lost a small but critical screw. The lost part prevented his spool from turning in either direction. It was effectively locked up. We were able to disassemble the reel well enough to get a workable length of fly line off the spool. John was able to finish out the day. Admittedly, it was a little cumbersome, but passably functional.

The reel is not a tool that is critical for catching more fish; however, a good reel gives you years of service and performs an important function in playing and landing fish. Its role is covered in chapter 6. The reel holds line, and it is important that it operates smoothly and balances your casting system.

Paintings and photographs of anglers casting midstream to rising trout show the graceful arc of the fly line silhouetted against the forested streamside. The curves of the line are pleasant images in front of the natural landscape. The most visually dramatic scene in the fly-fishing flick *A River Runs Through It* was that of Brad Pitt's character, Paul Maclean, casting while standing atop a rock. It is depicted as the most beautiful and graceful art of angling, and it is!

Watching a good fly caster is like watching an artist. The line cuts through the air, forward and backward, in fluid S-curves. If the fly rod is the angler's brush, then the line is the color as it is laid on the palette. It is both artistic and productive.

The fly line is the second link in the connection between angler and fish. It is the fly line's weight that you cast. It smoothly pulls the fly through the air to the target destination. A good quality and well-maintained fly line serves the fly-fishing predator. The fly line should be stretched and cleaned to provide you with the best performance. A clean and un-frayed line slides through the guides on the rod easier and smoother, giving you better distance and accuracy.

After power is imparted to the line from the rod, much of the energy is lost through air friction and the ever-present pull of gravity. The key to effective presentation is applying the correct amount of power to achieve the distance needed. Application of this principle is covered in chapter 5.

The fly line is your best friend or your worst enemy when it comes to drag on the fly. You can fight it or you can control it to your advantage. Wind may be the villain, but the fly line is your weapon against wind. Learn to deal with it.

Fly lines give you predator advantage!

The delicate lines in a painting draw you into the texture and depth of the strokes. Subtleties give richness to the art. The leader is the subtlest tool in the fly-fishing system.

One warm, sunny summer day, my fishing partner was sneaking up on a feeding brown trout. The fish was holding under the end of a log that had fallen into the slow-flowing run. There were no ripples on the water to disguise the presentation of the tiny dry fly. He cast. The Size 20 Adams extended to the end of the 7x tapered leader and floated gently on the surface two feet above the fish. The trout, not noticing or suspecting anything out of the ordinary, sipped in the fly. After landing the chunky trout and releasing it back into the clear water, he looked up and said, "I'm sure glad these skinny leaders don't spook off the fish!"

Leaders make you sneaky. They are smaller in diameter than your fly line, which reduces fish-frightening impact on the water's surface. They are softer than the fly line and less affected by the pull of the currents, allowing the fly to drift more naturally. They are stretchy and add to the shock absorbency of your system. They are translucent and less noticeable to fish.

There are varied schools of thought about leaders, from level to manufactured taper to knotted, with step-down progressions in diameter. Like rods and fly lines, the type of leader you use should be based on personal preference.

The leader is the tool that completes the link in the transference of power from the angler to the fly. The energy should terminate at the end of the leader and deliver the fly gracefully to the proper spot. The leader is the critical link between the relatively bulky and invasive fly line and the delicate fly of choice.

Leaders give you predator advantage!

Flies are art in and of themselves. Delicate materials are attached to hooks by the hands of artisans. The colors and proportions are pleasing to the eye. The fly is the ultimate charlatan. It is the tool designed to fool the fish into visualizing food. It is the final connection from the predator to the prey.

There are varied schools of thought about fly selection. There are anglers who only fish with a few patterns in a limited number of sizes. There are anglers who know the Latin names of all the natural insects that inhabit our rivers, and they have thousands of sophisticated imitations to mimic each. The fly-fishing predator just wants to improve his odds on catching fish. A discussion about fly imitation and selection strategy is covered in chapter 4.

Flies give you predator advantage!

As you wander the aisles of your favorite fly shop or pore over the slick pages and descriptions of a catalog, you will discover an infinite array of things to add to your arsenal. Even though many of them facilitate angling tasks, or add to your information about the sport, or organize you in an innovative and different way, or make you more comfortable, or just seem cool, most of them are just peripheral to your predator needs. But two of these seemingly peripheral tools—waders and tackle pack/vests—allow the angler to become a better fly-fishing predator and improve their experience.

Watch an angler work a stream without waders. He must hug one side of a river and only try for a small percentage of the fish available or get wet. Sometimes, the best angling spots are on the opposite side of the stream. When obstacles like trees, brush, and boulders inhibit his progress, he must bushwhack inland to get around them.

Waders provide you with dry comfort while giving you the flexibility of greater movement. They let you move through the water, side to side, and upstream and downstream, which can improve your angle of attack. As a predator, you want to alter your position so you will have more opportunities to improve your odds of success.

Waders give you predator advantage!

Effective hunters are constantly on the move. It is more convenient to carry your supplies than to go back to a tackle box every time you need something. A tackle pack or vest keeps your flies, leaders, floatant, nippers, and other tools within easy reach. Having your paraphernalia close at hand gives you the option of shifting tactics and tools as conditions change.

Tackle packs or vests give you predator advantage!

Understanding the tools of the trade is your first step in becoming a fly-fishing predator. ■

CHAPTER TWO

Sharpen Your Casting Skills

A foot-long rainbow trout moves from his hiding spot tucked next to the bank of a river to the faster current. Fifty feet in the air, an osprey rides thermals with its five-foot wingspan. From his vantage point, no glare on the water's surface impedes his vision. When the rainbow moves into its feeding lane, the fish hawk sees it. The bird hovers then dives. Just prior to hitting the water, he thrusts his legs forward and folds his wings back, plunging feet-first into the river. Ospreys are effective predators. They catch fish on about 50 percent of their dives. In seconds, their brains calculate the distance to their prey, the optimum direction of attack, wind speed and direction, the speed of the current, how deep in the river their prey is holding, and the effects of refraction. You must hone your skills in these same areas in order to be more effective. This chapter is about sharpening your casting skills. You already have basic casting ability, now your goal is to improve your command of the cast to become a better fly-fishing predator. My friend Bill and I were fishing a small New Mexico stream one beautiful fall afternoon. The sky was blue, the trees awash with golds, oranges, and reds, the stream water crystal clear and the fish feeding on newly hatched mayflies. Bill worked a nice run on his side of the river. The flow concentrated into a narrow trough, dropping into a scoured channel that ran under deadfall that had accumulated over the summer.

Bill aimed for a feeding brown trout. His cast required absolute control over distance. If he cast short, the fly would land behind the trout. If he cast long, the fly would tangle in the matrix of branches.

Bill is an accomplished fly-fishing predator. His cast landed the fly inches from the tangle of sticks and right in front of the trout's nose. The fish took the imitation and Bill landed and released the handsome fish.

Too often when fly-fishing enthusiasts talk about casting distance, they get all worked up over how far they can cast. Admittedly, having the ability to cast seventy, eighty, or even a hundred feet is to your advantage. However, to be an effective fly-fishing predator, most of your casting ranges will be less than fifty feet, and the twenty-foot cast will be the most common.

Controlling casting distance is critical to improving your effectiveness. When fish settle into feeding positions, they may not swim far to intercept your fly. You will run into occasions when trout will not even drift a foot in either direction. That's why it is all the more important to bring the fly to them.

There are skill exercises described in fly-casting books and fly-fishing magazines. Pick one, put in practice time, and reap the rewards. Regardless of which practice technique you choose, you should be able to consistently place a fly within the space of a dinner platter twenty feet away.

Learning to control your distance helps you avoid trouble. There always seems to be overhanging brush, driftwood sticks, piles of rocks, and logjams in rivers that fish just love to hang around. Casting into these holding areas produces more fish if you control where the fly lands.

A villain of reducing these precise takes is drag. When fly lines or leaders exert pressure on the fly, it causes the fly to move in odd directions from the current. Sometimes it can also cause the fly to travel at a different speed than the natural flow of the water. These deviations are unnatural activity for insects, which you are trying to mimic, and the movement reduces or eliminates strikes. But if you control the distance in your casts, you also control the negative effects of drag.

A considerable challenge to controlling your distance is wind. You will be faced with casts when the wind is in your face, coming from behind your back, or coming across your body from every conceivable direction. Learning to cope with these nuances improves your ability to catch more fish.

Controlling your distance gives you predator advantage!

Jim was a novice. One day, he was standing in the tail-out of a nice little hole with fish feeding on the left side of the current, very close to the bank. The trout were within his casting reach, but he was having difficulty getting his fly into the correct drift line. His fly landed in the middle of the current, then in the flat water to the right of the current, and then up the grassy streamside. His shoulders drooped. His casting distance was working, but his direction failed him.

The ability to manage the direction of your casts improves your predator success.

As you work a river, you see things. You see where two tongues of current come together, creating an ideal funnel to bring food to waiting fish. You see fish rising near undercut banks. You see brush and tree limbs hanging over deep holes, with fish feeding in the shadows. You see your own shadow falling on the surface in front of you. You see fish holding in flat water above a jumble of rocks.

The most important aspect of controlling your direction is getting the fly to land in the place that will catch the most fish. Obviously, this skill is combined with your ability to control your distance. Like distance, controlling for direction comes from practice. You should be able to control your direction within about six inches to either side of your target. There are times when even that range is not accurate enough, but for the most part, such accuracy will serve you well.

As you recall from the first chapter, one of the tools that is beneficial, but not necessary, to fly-fishing is a pair of waders. Wading gives you the predator advantage of mobility. You can shift from one side of the river to the other or work your way right up the middle of the river. In many cases, the way to avoid casting hindrances is to shift your position of attack.

When you see fish feeding along an undercut bank, you want to approach it from the direction that gives you a natural drift without contending with crosscurrents. Often the best angle is on the same side of the river the bank is on and directly below it.

Tree limbs overhanging the river create all kinds of challenges for the angler. Primarily, they make it is easy to get your fly and leader hopelessly tangled. You have two choices when this happens. You can break off the fly, re-rig, and try again, or you can wade into the hole and disengage your fly from the tangle. Either way, the odds of you putting fish down (spooking them) are high.

Fish are wary of their predators. Any time shadows fall on the water, their survival instincts kick in. They are cautious of every unnatural movement within their sensory range. You must avoid your shadow creeping anywhere between you and the fish. Ignoring this rule causes them to bolt from the area. Another advantage of using waders is that you can move to a new position to eliminate your shadow entering the water, thereby increasing your chances of catching fish.

Like an osprey, a fly-fishing predator must always be aware of his profile, his movement, and his shadow.

Another factor to consider when controlling for direction is reducing the effect of glare on the river. Glare renders you blind when it comes to seeing your fly on the water. But by moving to one side or the other and controlling the direction of your cast, you neutralize the problem.

As I have already mentioned, the effect of drag on your fly ruins any other part of the presentation. Drag turns fish off. Because there are so many variables in the way currents flow, one of your main tasks is to reduce or eliminate the potential causes of drag. The benefit of direction control is that you manage drag on the fly before it happens.

Controlling the direction of your casts gives you predator advantage.

Todd saw fish feeding along the rocky shoreline. The feeding line the fish were working was slow compared to the speed of the water just a foot out from the edge. Every time Todd cast, the fly landed near the correct spot, but the fly line landed in faster water, which immediately pulled the fly away from its drifting line. It did not put the fish down, but the trout did not take the fly, either. After three unsuccessful presentations, Todd asked how to deal with this situation. I told him to cock his casting plane forty-five degrees and try again. When he made the next cast, the momentum of the fly curved the leader. The fly landed gently next to the rocks. The fly hesitated in that spot for a few seconds without moving while the current took the slack out of the fly line. Before the pull on the line caused drag on the fly, the trout tipped its nose up and inhaled the fly. Todd landed the chunky, twelve-inch brown and learned a valuable lesson about curves.

Similar to controlling distance and direction, learning to master curves gives you three predator advantages:

- You can present a fly in such a way that fish see the fly before they discern the leader, which prompts more strikes.

- You can cast around interfering objects to reach difficult lies.

- You reduce the effects of drag on the fly line, which keeps the fly in the fish's window longer.

Fish are perceptive. They are on constant alert for their predators. Anything that appears as out of the ordinary assaults their senses. A fly line cast over their

By tilting the rod 45° to perpendicular, the author can curve a cast underneath tree limbs overhanging a fish-holding spot.

holding spot sends them scurrying to cover. Leaders that catch light in strange ways put them on guard. A fly that is followed by a coiled leader when it hits the water inhibits takes.

Learning to curve the last few feet of your leader reduces leader fright. It puts the fly in the fish's window before it notices the leader. Curves give you advantage on nearly every cast.

As you work up any stream, you will be confronted with obstacles. Rocks interfere with your line of casting. Streamside vegetation gets in the way. Limbs from deadfall jammed into makeshift dams create perfect holding spots for trout and chaos for you. Combined with distance and direction, controlling curves brings even more trout into play for your fly. You cannot make obstacles go away, but curves let you fish more productive water.

Every stream is a puzzle of multiple currents. A number of these currents are detectable to the angler, but many are still impossible to see. The variation of different currents is one of the major culprits causing drag on your fly line, which in turn

Luther Wilson kneels on the bank to make his predator presentation in a nice spot.

unnaturally moves your fly. Controlling curves nullifies drag and makes every cast more effective.

Learning how to control your curves can come from casting books or lessons from a trained instructor. An easy way to begin your curve control is shifting the plane of your casts.

When conditions are good, you cast with a perpendicular rod to the water. Your line snakes forward and back, directly over your head. To curve a cast to the right, shift your casting plane forty-five degrees to the left. When the fly reaches the end of the cast, the last few feet of leader curve. When you shift your plane forty-five degrees to the right, it results in a left curve of the last few feet of leader.

When you control distance, direction, and curves in your casting, you present your fly to more fish more effectively. The more fish you present it to, the more you catch.

Controlling curves gives you predator advantage.

Once you master these skills, your fishing effectiveness will greatly improve. But to really become the best fly-fishing predator you can be, you will have to add a few perceptive skills to your repertoire:

Develop intuition. After a few years of fly-fishing, you develop a gut feeling about where fish are holding and what kind of cast you need in order to give yourself the best chance of catching them.

Develop imagination. Take a survey of all the variables in a particular fish's holding area. Use your imagination to combine multiple casting skills and tools in an imaginative way to reach more fish. Imagination is a powerful tool.

Develop innovation. Try something new. The adage applies: "If you always do what you always did, you will always get what you always got." Innovation is applying the skills and techniques you know in new and different ways to solve problems. No two days of fishing are the same, nor will two fish ever be in exactly the same spot. You should always strive for improvement in your presentation.

Sharpening your casting skills gives you predator advantage. ■

CHAPTER THREE

Sharpen Your Ability to Read the Water

A lioness moves with care through the early morning shadows cast by jungle trees. She skirts the watering hole, searching for food to feed her hungry cubs. After many years, she has learned that easy prey frequent this pool to drink. Through her experience, she maximizes her chances for a successful hunt.

Just as the lioness learns to hunt specific, productive places, so too the fly-fishing predator must learn the best potential spots for catching fish. Through reading the water, you can identify what an underwater environment looks like relative to your observations of the water's surface characteristics. The better you read the water, imagine the subsurface structure of the

river, and therefore understand where the fish are most likely positioned, the better your chances for a successful hunt.

You must first understand fish's requirements for survival. They need food, safety, and energy conservation. Fish must keep these three basic needs in balance or risk their survival.

As with all living creatures, fish require food. Fish are a predator species, too. They adapted their diet to the foodstuff that floats on the surface of water, is suspended in the water column, or crawls on the bottom of a stream or lake. Fish must be able to get sustenance on a continuous basis or perish.

Even though fish are predators, they are also prey. They have many natural enemies, and they require protection from these predators. Their natural camouflage and swimming ability provide them with some protection. They also benefit from stream structure and water depth to preserve their safety.

Fish must reside in an environment where they can maintain positive energy conservation. That is, they must be able to take in more calories through their captured prey than they expend in the chase. Food is carried to fish's holding spots by the current. These morsels vary in size and quantity. Depth, rate of flow, oxygen content, and temperature affect fish's metabolism. The relationship between fish's intake of foodstuff and their metabolic rate determines their ability to flourish.

Prime holding spots have a balance of all three of these survival requirements. The most dominant and typically the largest fish hold the best spots.

As you prowl the rivers and streams, you want to cast your fly into the best possible place to catch fish. The easiest scenario is to find fish actively feeding. When fish are feeding on the surface, they signal their position. It is simple logic to cast your fly to reach their feeding position. It is important to note that when fish are aggressively feeding, they may compromise their other survival requirements for a period of time. But they often will not reveal themselves, so you must rely on your predatory skills.

Fish face into the current, and this is for two critical reasons. First, water must flow through their mouths and across their gills in order for them to extract life-giving oxygen. Second, the current is their primary resource for food. Fish hold their position and capture food that is suspended on or in the water. Insects are fish's primary diet, and they often intercept them in the flow.

You must develop the ability to interpret visual surface variations as clues to the underwater hydromorphology. In simpler terms, the character of the water surface helps you imagine the form and structure of the fish's underwater world. When you understand what this underwater world looks like and how the fish are likely to react to different environments, then you are better prepared to be more productive as a fly-fishing predator.

This is a classic-looking trout stream. It is the fly-fishing predator's skill that will, with visual clues, find the fish.

Water character varies constantly throughout the river. It is normal to find several characteristics occurring side by side or concurrently. Your goal is to recognize the distinct features of the surface and proceed to work your fly to where you expect the fish will be.

Primary Current Direction

The force of gravity pulls water downward. It follows the fall line of the terrain and flows steadily from higher to lower elevation. This is the primary current direction.

Since fish face into the current, fly-fishing predators move upstream most of the time. Cast your fly to land on the water above or upstream from where you imagine fish are holding. This puts your fly into the fish's natural feeding lane, allowing the current to bring it downstream to waiting mouths.

Fish see in a front-facing view that spans about 270 degrees. Because you are wading and casting upstream—the direction the fish are facing—you are effectively hiding in their blind spot. This gives you predator advantage.

Central flow is obvious in this run. The line of bubbles are a dead giveaway to where the deepest part of the channel flows.

Central Flow

In any stretch of river, there is a central flow. This is where the majority of the stream's water volume concentrates. Under normal circumstances, it is flowing at the fastest rate. The speed of this current dictates how and where the fish will position themselves and how they feed.

When current speed is high, it reduces the number of fish that feed in this main channel. Even though the central flow holds a lot of food, the negative trade-off is the energy it requires to remain in such a fast current may not be worth the gain in nutrition. Not only does it take a great amount of energy to simply hold their position, but it also requires an additional burst of energy for them to chase food.

Where there is a fairly high-speed central flow, fish sit in the slower water of the river's edges. This conserves energy while still providing them the opportunity to dart into the main current to pick off food.

If the central current is not moving at a high speed, it is an ideal place for the fish

As the current flows into this hole, the terrain pushes the water to swing along the left bank of cliffs.

to lurk. They can hold their position easily while maximizing their food intake. Fish in this moderate-speed flow sit directly in the middle of the river and move straight up or off to either side of the current to capture insects.

The central flow offers the additional advantage of deeper water. In fact, the central flow is often the deepest part of the river. This deeper and more turbulent water provides the fish with the added benefit of protection from their predators.

Swings

As water seeks its natural course and forges the streambed, the main current swings from bank to bank, resulting in the curves and meanders of a river. When this main flow encounters the embankment, it changes direction back to the center of the stream-bed. This swing creates a deeper channel on that side, providing better holding spots for fish, especially at the bend. The water speed at this bend slows before veering off in a different direction.

This is a well-defined run that maintains a distinctive central flow.

Food concentrates as it squeezes into narrow bands at the bend. Since this water slows, it makes an easy and productive banquet for the fish.

The scouring pressure of water as it makes this turn results in carved-out undercuts. This underwater formation provides protection from the fish's predators. Slower water along the edges allows fish to hold their position and conserve energy.

Depending on the subsurface morphology, fish may hold on either side of the bend. If water along the bankside edges slows and gouges out a cavern, fish hold all along the bend with an eye toward the food line. If there is adequate depth on the inside of the curve, fish congregate in this slower water and feed along the edge of the current.

Runs

A run is a segment of the central flow. When water tumbles from an elevated and shallower area and the structure of the streambed concentrates the water into a lower, narrower, and deeper channel, it creates a run. Runs consist of three parts, and fish may be in any or all of the parts.

A plunge pool at the head of a run.

The head of the run is the uppermost section. Steep grade increases water speed, and as it funnels into a lower elevation, it gouges out a deeper cavity. Water is more turbulent in this part of the run. Fish reside in this part of the stream when they can find a spot where the water slows, especially in the plunge pool, where the water sits before continuing on its downstream course. Fish sit with their noses tucked right up to the churning water.

After the water creates these small plunge pools, the stream spreads out and continues down the channel, creating the heart of the run. There, water current is moderate and the river's depth maintains for some distance before the stream shallows out again. This is ideal water for fish. The depth here provides some protection from predators. The current moves the food along at a leisurely pace, giving the fish easy pickings and positive energy conservation. Fish hold anywhere in the heart of the run, but they closely watch the foam line of the river because this is where most of the food is concentrated. If there is no obvious foam line, fish sit along the edges of the central current.

Water drops from a higher elevation into a plunge pool.

Right where the water drops, a turbulent hole is carved out. Seldom are there fish in this spot.

When the water begins to flatten, especially in a shaded area, fish will congregate.

As the main flow of the current begins to subside, you may find fish stacked up.

When a current flows at a uniform depth over a gravel bottom, a riffle is liable to hold fish anywhere.

As the stream widens and shallows, the water surface flattens. The tail-out of a run is the short distance between the heart and the beginnings of another type of water characteristic. When fish are aggressively feeding, especially during prolific insect activity, the tail-out is very productive. The shallow and flat water increases visibility into the stream. This clarity makes the fish far more susceptible to their predators, so they often hold in a spot that affords them a quick getaway to deeper, more turbulent positions. When insects are plentiful, fish compromise their protection to maximize their food intake.

Runs are productive places to prospect for fish.

Riffle

Moderate-speed current flowing over a relatively uniform gravel and rock-strewn streambed creates a choppy water surface. Water surface tension is broken in places, causing splashes. Oxygen concentration increases, which provides good conditions for both fish and insects.

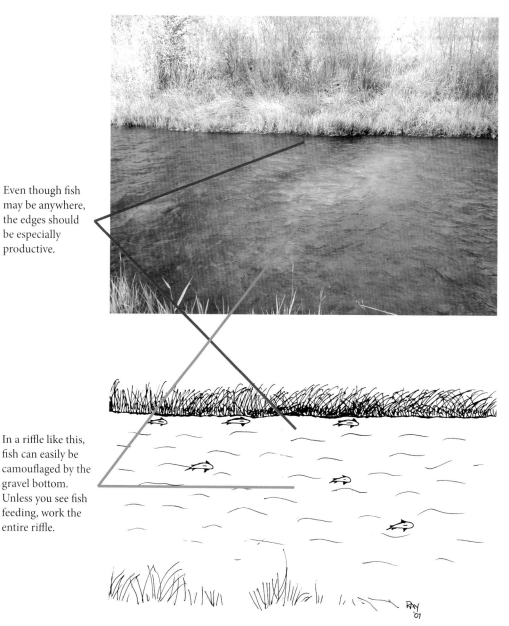

Even though fish may be anywhere, the edges should be especially productive.

In a riffle like this, fish can easily be camouflaged by the gravel bottom. Unless you see fish feeding, work the entire riffle.

Rocky bottoms are tremendous backdrops for fish's camouflage markings, which makes them very hard for predators to perceive. Fish tuck along the sides of rocks and feed anywhere across the riffle. Oftentimes, larger fish hang toward the bottom end of a riffle, capturing hatching insects suspended in the current.

Pocket water is created when there is a steady current broken up by exposed rocks or submerged rock piles.

Pocket Water

A riffle containing large rocks and small boulders that may protrude above the water's surface is called pocket water. Each of these protruding or near-surface boulders creates a deeper pocket of water directly downstream from the obstruction.

Pockets are ideal spots for fish to hold. In them, they are protected from predators, and the water immediately below the rocks slows, affording the fish energy-efficient resting areas and rendering a collection basin for food.

When you are fishing pockets, cast a short line directly into the pocket without letting the current drag your fly downstream. Maintain only the fly and a small section of leader on the water.

Another feature of pocket water often missed by anglers is directly upstream of these protruding boulders. As flowing water bumps against one of these boulders, it backs up before it is deflected around the impediment. In this backed-up area, fish easily hold and pick off insects that enter this flat zone. Drop your fly upstream and let it drift into the space. Once again, you must allow only the fly and a few inches of tippet to remain in contact with the water to avoid drag.

Pocket water holds a lot of fish, making it an important hunting ground for predator fly-fishing.

When water depth is maintained, the edges will hold fish. The near side of this run is shallow and you shouldn't find fish there.

White water tumbling over rock piles are great indicators of deeper pockets just below them.

Boulders that obstruct the flow are ideal spots for fish. Fish may hold both below and above this type of obstacle.

Water funnels between two rock piles, creating a channel that should hold fish.

As the current swings into a grass-covered bank, it undercuts the roots and carves out wonderful trout habitat.

Undercut Bank

Undercut banks created by water pressure are the result of swing. When the flow of the stream runs into a grassy bank, it erodes soil underneath root-reinforced ground. The impact of the water excavates an underwater cavern that harbors trout.

Because it prohibits easy perception or access to fish, overhanging sod provides ideal protection from predators. Water slows, allowing for both good energy conservation and prime conditions for feeding.

Remember that trout tuck up under the bank, so your fly must be right on the edge of the current and shore. You must be very cautious in your approach to undercut banks, especially when you are on the bank itself. Heavy footfalls may cause vibrations to transfer from the ground into the water. Tread lightly.

Side Channels

As a stream seeks its course, occasionally a segment of river splits from the main flow and creates a side channel. This side channel may have any of the characteristics discussed in this chapter—just on a smaller scale.

Where the current is the strongest, you will not normally find fish.

The undercut band may be deepest right where the channel begins its turn. This is a great spot for fish.

As the current wanes, fish will hold in this spot to capture the varied fare the river pushes to this side. The overhanging grasses provide protection from the fish's overhead predators.

If its water volume is meager, it may not hold any fish at all. If its water volume is sufficient, you may find some of the nicest fish in the stream taking advantage of this sidebar environment.

Counter Currents

The shore's frictional forces cause current to turn back on itself and flow in the opposite direction from the primary current.

Eddies are the most obvious of the counter currents. In them, water swirls and appears to be flowing in continuous circles. Often, foam collects on the surface in these backflows, forming a floating mat. This cover provides excellent protection for fish.

Counter currents, considerably slower than the normal flow, provide great energy conservation positions. Insects caught in the foam are easy pickings for the fish.

Fishing counter currents can be tricky because of the fish's holding position. As you recall, fish need to face into the current; so in this situation, they may be looking straight downriver. If you make traditional approaches from downstream, the fish may easily spot you.

In the preceding pages, you have learned about the primary streamflow characteristics along with where, within those types of water, you might expect to find fish. In the next section, three more well-defined features that are especially recognized for holding fish will be revealed. These features are normally found in conjunction with the primary characteristics we just covered. Fly-fishing predators pay additional attention to these features.

Junction Boxes

As water finds its course, it deflects around objects in streams such as boulders, trees, and islands. Where the flow merges back together is called a junction box. Or, if two currents are only separated by underwater obstructions, the confluence of these currents is also called a junction box.

Just upstream of where two currents mingle, flatter and slower water occurs. This is an optimal spot for fish. It affords protection because the water's surface breaks up, making it difficult for predators to see into the water. It also renders a quiet current for positive energy conservation—and as a bonus for the fish, the two currents carry more food past the holding position.

Flies cast into junction boxes produce a lot of fish.

The river has split around a gravel bar, creating two currents that swing into the right bank. Fish will hold below and above the confluence of the lower flow.

Seams

Water moves at different speeds in different parts of a stream. Where two different flows abut, seams appear. Fish love to hang in these seams. Slower-flowing water gives fish good energy conservation positions, while swifter currents bring food.

Concentrate on seams and catch more fish.

Slicks

Slicks form in a variety of ways. Underwater structure causes water to flatten with very little current. These smooth spots give fish good holding positions. They settle into these areas because the surrounding current provides food and protection while the holding area does not drain their energy.

Insects concentrate into these flat areas, providing a smorgasbord for fish. Slicks are good hunting grounds for fly-fishing predators because they are good hunting grounds for the fish.

Up to this point, variations in the current composed the major topic in this book. Underwater geomorphology and the effects of hydrology cause these variations. Barriers causing the flow to change direction or speed create fish holding spots. In the next section, these barriers get a closer look.

Midstream boulders divert the central flow in many areas. Fish are attracted to this break in the current.

Rocks, stumps, logs, logjams, and islands cause deflection in the natural direction of currents. As flowing water collides with objects, the water backs up before advancing on a new course around those impediments. Hydraulic action creates scooped-out depressions downstream where slower water gathers before continuing. This slower water preserves fish's energy and slows food suspended in the current.

Boulders
These large barriers sit along the edges of rivers or in midstream. Anytime a swift current diverts around boulders, it creates a good holding spot downstream.

Rocks
Rocks are smaller than boulders and larger than gravel. They are the building blocks of pocket water. A riffle is the result of a relatively consistent streambed. When there is a scattering of rocks, fish-holding pocket water develops.

Fish hold behind many of these rocks and feed on passing fare. Pocket water contains more fish than most anglers expect. Fly-fishing predators work all the pockets carefully.

You will notice the steep hillside on the left side of the river. This slope should continue down into the river, creating a nice, deep run along this side.

Where the water slows behind the boulder is a hole that has been scoured out. This is a tremendous spot for fish.

As currents reconverge, fish will settle in along these seams.

Logs and debris channel the flow of the stream. Nice holding spots for trout are created below these drop-offs.

Downfall Trees

Nature has a way of improving fish's environment. Aging, insect infestation, or beaver forage causes trees to fall into rivers. Fish reside and feed around trunks and branches that interfere with the flow of the river due to the protection they provide and the reduced current speed nearby them.

Fishing a downfall is precarious, but a proficient caster reaps the rewards.

Logjams

Spring runoff moves a lot of material around, especially logs, limbs, and branches. This material gets caught on in-stream boulders, rocks, or other fallen trees, creating makeshift dams that back up the flow. These dams create slower and deeper pools, providing good fish lairs.

Naturally created logjams and beaver dams are built from the same materials. Each improves the quality of the fishery. Below these dams, water scours out depressions that are ideal fish habitats.

Ply the water up to the base of the dam, working your fly along every finger of current. Once you exhaust these opportunities, cast your fly into the pool above

This hole offers a variety of possibilities.

the dam. Keep a low profile because the fish in these pools are acutely aware of danger-ous movement.

Understanding stream hydromorphology is important when sharpening your abil-ity to read the water. Get familiar with additional factors that come into play as you become a fly-fishing predator. Each of the following elements impacts where fish rest or fish's behavior.

Depth

As water depth increases, the river's color changes. Increased depth (and therefore darker water) provides more protection. Larger fish seek out deeper areas. When water is very deep, it is difficult for fly anglers to fish it without special equipment and tech-niques. The advantage fly-fishing predators have is realized when fish move from deep water into shallower positions to feed.

Water in the deeper part of a run moves slower than the surface flow. This is benefi-cial to fish's energy conservation.

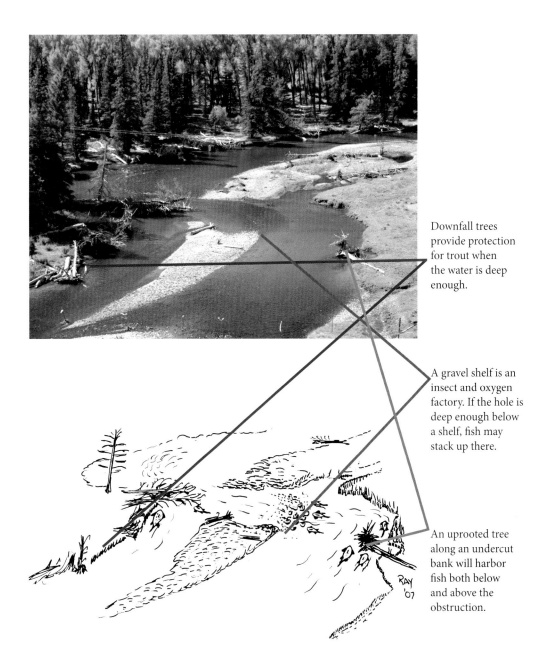

Downfall trees provide protection for trout when the water is deep enough.

A gravel shelf is an insect and oxygen factory. If the hole is deep enough below a shelf, fish may stack up there.

An uprooted tree along an undercut bank will harbor fish both below and above the obstruction.

Color

Environmental factors also alter water color and clarity. In a freestone river, spring snowmelt changes the stream's color for extended periods. Rain anywhere along the river's drainage basin can discolor the water. Fish react to these changing conditions.

Most rivers run low and clear during winter months. As seasons change to warmer weather, high country snowpack melts and discharges material-laden water into the flow. There are three distinctive periods of snowmelt.

During early runoff, the water temperature is still cold, and increased flow causes water to discolor from debris carried to the stream by surface runoff from the initial melted snow. Fish are still lethargic due to low water temperatures, but it is during this first influx of volume that they begin a more active feeding regimen. They move to the edges of the stream and pick off aquatic insect nymphs that also get more active during this time of year.

In the height of spring runoff, rivers swell with higher flows and water that runs muddy brown. Fishing during this phase is generally unproductive. High, discolored water causes fish to sulk and feed sparingly.

In late spring to early summer, runoff wanes and flows begin to return to normal. Water color shifts from chocolate brown to different degrees of murky and then eventually back to clear. During this period, water temperatures begin increasing, spawning more insect activity, which in turn creates more fish feeding activity. Fishing during this period is often the best out of the year. Fish gorge themselves on insects, launching the fish's summer growth period.

As summer rainsqualls pellet the surrounding area, the ground's surface becomes saturated. Excess water that cannot be absorbed by the soil runs off and fuels the river. This excess water carries loose material into the river, causing discolored water. As it does in spring runoff conditions, the range of this roil varies, but it typically only lasts a few hours to a few days. If the rains do not turn the color of the river to the color of your morning coffee, fishing can be fantastic.

Slightly off-color water provides fish added security from their predators, so they lose some of their caution in these conditions. This makes them more susceptible to the fly-fishing predator.

Time of Day

The angle of the sun's rays on the surface of a river impacts fish's eating habits. Fish prefer low-angled light conditions for the majority of their feeding activity because it is more difficult for their predators to see them in it. Early morning is an ideal time for fish to forage. Long shadows are cast on the east side of streams and fish congregate toward these shaded areas.

During midday hours, the sun's angle is directly overhead. The sun's rays, which are then perpendicular to the surface of the water, expose every detail of the stream's bottom. Fish become warier during this bright-light period.

As the sun approaches the western horizon late in the day, long shadows and low-angled rays again prevail. This time, the shaded areas are on the western edge of the river. Fish migrate to that side.

Seasons

The seasons do not affect how you read the water. But as a fly-fishing predator, they do affect where fish are in the watershed and how their eating habits will vary. The following discussion is pertinent to the freestone streams. Tail-water fisheries are not as affected by the season as free-flowing rivers.

Spring

Not only does warmer weather cause trees to leaf and flowers to bloom, it also perks up fish's appetite. They practically hibernate during the winter months without taking in much nutrition . . . and in the spring their hunger is sparked.

As the water warms, fish become more active. Early morning and early evening temperatures remain low, so your best fishing occurs between 8 a.m. and 6 p.m.

Summer

Water and air temperatures increase. Water temperatures exceeding 65 degrees cause a reduction in oxygen content in rivers. It also causes fish's metabolism to decrease. This slows their activity and inhibits eating habits.

Water volumes decrease, causing greater exposure to predators.

Fishing is better in low-light conditions. Fish from dawn up to 10 a.m. and from 5 p.m. until dark for best results.

Fall

As cooler weather sets in, water temperatures also cool, stimulating renewed fish activity.

Fish's feeding exertion increases as they prepare for leaner winter periods.

Fish all day.

Winter

Water volume and water temperatures drop as the days become shorter and winter weather sets in. Water clarity is at its greatest, making fish extremely susceptible to their predators. Fish metabolism decreases, inducing lethargy. They hold in the deepest, quietest spots of rivers and eat sparingly.

Fishing is typically slow. Fish from 10 a.m. to 4 p.m. when the water is warm enough.

Hydromorphology is the way flowing water carves the riverbed and creates the variety of underwater environs where the fish love to live and feed. Learning to read the water is critical to your success. The lioness's experiences make her an efficient predator. When you sharpen your ability to read the water, you become a better fly-fishing predator. ■

CHAPTER FOUR

Sharpen Your Instincts
for Choosing a Fly

The great blue heron stands immobile, a sooty-gray statue fixed among cattails grow-ing in shallows along the edge of the pond. His experience and instinct suggest that his prey will be in range shortly. Like miniature star flashes, a silvery sparkle briefly appears over the water-covered roots of cattails growing in the shadows. A minnow searching for food probes the bottom muck, oblivious to the nearby danger. As the minnow swims into the heron's reach, the great bird snaps his head toward the small fish and snatches up his meal.

Experience along with natural instinct serves this predator well. These same two elements will provide the fly-fishing predator with the tools needed to improve fly selection in the search for his quarry.

The world of fish is filled with material objects mixed in the water. Trout survive by discerning food items from other debris suspended in the current. Through trial and error, fish improve their ability to distinguish flotsam from potential nutrition. Over time, they get better at this survival skill. The more finely tuned they are at distinguishing food, the greater the challenge they pose for the angler. This is why larger, older fish are typically more selective and difficult to catch.

During the course of the year, the abundance of one type of insect or other food form exceed others. We know, for example, that certain insect species will hatch in the early spring and not in the fall. Conversely, there are bugs that will not come out until the water is warmed by the midsummer sun. Likewise, throughout a day or even within a few hours, there will be more of a particular insect present than others. For instance, adult caddisflies may not be present in the early part of the day, but come late afternoon, the water may be blanketed by them. This phenomenon is commonly called "hatches," but that term frequently includes pre-hatch activity, hatching itself, delayed hatching activity due to weather conditions, ovipositing, and the spent stage after mating. At any rate, as the number of a particular insect increases, that species becomes more available to fish.

When a fly-fishing predator is at streamside, it is important for him or her to recognize that at a particular point in time, trout are exposed to a specific prey more than others. As a result of this peak of a particular insect or insect stage, if only for a limited time, trout may key on this food source. Often adding to this challenge is the fact that fish in one type of water may be keying on a different insect or insect stage than fish in other types of flow during the same period.

For example, caddisfly adults may be ovipositing in the riffle portion of the stream. These insects are active flyers that bob and dip. Often they splash land on the surface to dislodge their eggs. They may skim in a zigzag path, leaving a wake behind them. As the bugs dip onto the water's surface to lay their eggs, pursuing trout slash at their prey, reacting quickly and with abandon. They demonstrate unselective, aggressive behavior in order to capture this fleeting prey. Below the riffles, where the water calms and runs quietly next to a grassy bank, spent adult caddisflies awash in the surface film are trapped and float nearly motionless. Fish in this area will gently sip these bugs and refuse anything that does not look or act like the real thing.

Offering the appropriate imitation puts the fly-fishing predator ahead in the hunt.

Common sense suggests that if there is a dominant number of a particular insect stage available to the trout, these trout will focus their attention and energy to capture as many of that form as they can to maximize their effort. The fish do not think about it; they just react to the stimulus. This is the rule of survival.

The fly-fishing predator hones his knowledge and experience, combining them with instinct to become more proficient.

Identifying the Naturals

There are hundreds of quality books and articles on this subject. The study of entomology can be a life's mission and profession. However, from a fly-fishing predator point of view, you need to only know the basics of identification. Then you can apply the predator skills of common sense and intuition.

You should be able to identify the common aquatic insects down to the family. These primarily include mayflies, caddisflies, stoneflies, and diptera. Most people can recognize the terrestrial insects that occasionally find their way into and onto water. These include grasshoppers, crickets, ants, and caterpillars. As easy and commonplace as it is to identify these terrestrial insects, it is no more difficult to identify aquatic insects. Familiarize yourself with both of these groups. Not only do appearances differ, but the characteristics and activity differ.

The mayfly is typically a small, delicate insect. The adult has upright wings when it is at rest.

The dry mayfly imitation should have a thin profile with upright wings.

The stonefly nymph crawls out onto a rock or streamside vegetation to metamorphose into the adult insect.

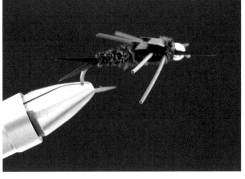

The stonefly nymph imitation should have similar properties to the natural. It should have a thick body with distinctive legs and wing pads.

Most adult stonefly insects are relatively large flies with four wings that fold over the back when at rest.

The dry stonefly pattern should be bushy and float down on the surface film. The laid-back wing provides the correct profile.

Midges hatch and swarm in prolific numbers. The fish are particularly interested in the insect's emerging stage.

An emerging midge pattern is fished just under the water's surface.

Terrestrial insects like this grasshopper often find themselves trapped in the surface film. They kick their hind legs in their effort to escape back to land.

A dry grasshopper pattern will float down in the surface film. A laid-back wing and distinctive rear legs offer a great temptation. The white post wing is for the angler, not the fish.

Some adult mayflies are trapped in this streamside web.

There are anglers who can key out insects down to the species' Latin name, such as *Baetis tricaudatus*. This becomes a study unto itself. The fly-fishing predator does not need to know the Latin name of the insect, just that it is a mayfly, one-half inch in length, with bluish-gray wings and an olive body color. It is those characteristics that will aid you in selecting an imitation.

Admittedly, the more you know about a subject, the better prepared you will be to deal with it. However, from a predator point of view, family, stage, size, and color give you the advantage necessary to improve your fly-selection efficiency.

Once you can identify the insects to the family level, even if using the common name rather than the scientific name, you can then improve your success by brushing up on streamside observation. Taking the time to collect and identify the bugs that are present enhances your success.

You may find natural insects or stages of these insects in a variety of places. When you first approach the stream, take note of the insects in the air. Capture a few and discover their type, size, and color. These are your first clues.

Another terrific spot to find insects that have been airborne in a recent period is to inspect spiderwebs that adorn streamside rocks, stems, and logs. This gives insight into which insects have been recently active. They may be different from what is now flying around the bushes.

Streamside shrubbery harbors insects that previously were airborne. These bugs may have just hatched or mated and are now resting in preparation for egg-laying activity.

It is important to note as you uncover these clues that just because you find insects in the air, the fish may not be keying on this phase. Look further. Lower your eyes to the water's surface. Insects may be floating on top or they may be in the surface film.

Flat-water edges along the shoreline may have a collection of the insects that were previously suspended in the film. They are collected into this flat water as living or recently deceased flotsam.

Just under the water's surface, insects are suspended in the water column between the surface and the streambed. These bugs may be preparing for their hatching period or they may just be an active type of insect.

Aquatic insects spend the vast majority of their lives as subsurface, gill-breathing, immature insects. These critters burrow in the muddy bottom, crawl between the bottom's substrate rock and gravel material, or attach themselves to submerged rocks, sticks, and logs. In your streamside observation, lift submerged rocks and sticks to discover the most numerous resident insects.

These observations provide you with a myriad of clues about the insects. They will point you in the right direction. The most valuable observation is seeing which insect and insect stage the fish are feeding on at that point in time. When you discover this, success is nearly assured.

Seasonality of the Naturals

There is seasonality to insect generations. As a group, they mature and react to stimuli uniformly. When the time is right, groups of the previously immature insects will transform into the adult, flying stage. Fish usually recognize the increased activity and sheer numbers of the insects and feed on the now more available insect form. This is called a hatch. Later, these mature insects mate and deposit eggs on or into the water to begin the cycle all over again. After ovipositing, many of these bugs perish and fall onto the water's surface. During this "fall," the insects are susceptible to the fish. Fish can consume large numbers in a fairly short period, which is a beneficial spike to their nutrient intake.

The annual (sometimes more frequent) schedule of each insect population is fairly predictable. As you spend more time on particular streams, you will learn these patterns and be prepared with proper imitations. Weather and water conditions may be factors. Even if you follow a schedule of appearance of a particular insect, adverse weather may delay or advance the natural's activity. Water condition, such as heavier or lighter flows, unseasonable temperatures, or temporary discoloration, may affect the insect's cycle by a few hours or even a few days.

Carry a good assortment of dry flies and nymphs
to improve your predation skills.

There are three interesting and entertaining hobbies I have already mentioned that can parallel your predator fly-fishing. They may add effectiveness and enjoyment to your pursuit.

The first is collecting natural insects at every stage of their development and mounting them for reference. This requires seining all levels of the water column, searching through the substrate that makes up the streambed, and chasing all sorts of flying insects. You will discover insects that cover the spectrum—from the rugged and clumsy stoneflies to the blue-collar caddisflies

These activities are intriguing in their own right and are a part of entomology. The important aspect about these concentrations of insects is that they tell you a lot about what fish are seeing. It provides you valuable information for your fly-fishing predator imitation selection.

Selecting an Imitation

There must be tens of thousands of patterns to choose from, with more being developed every day. The predator has a strategy for choosing a fly pattern to fish with each time he or she enters a stream.

to the delicate and graceful mayflies to the miniscule diptera. It is remarkable to discover the diversity each stream can offer.

Once you have experienced collecting, it may lead to two other off-stream activities—keying out for identification and fly tying.

Keying out for identification takes you into the field of entomology and observation through microscopes. It requires scientific discipline. A few anglers pursue this study and enjoy the satisfaction of knowledge gained.

More anglers get into fly tying than scientific entomology by a

The first step is to try to determine on which insect and insect stage you believe the fish are feeding. This is a combination of streamside observation as well as an understanding of the natural's activity traits and the season's and specific day's water and weather conditions. Visiting your local fly shop before venturing onto a stream provides valuable starting information. You can refine the details once your observation skills are utilized.

Once you decide which insect and insect stage you think the fish are keying on, look to patterns that imitate the natural's profile or silhouette. Is the natural a mayfly with upright wings, or is it a caddisfly with folded back wings? Do the naturals have the thin, delicate bodies of a mayfly or the thicker and stouter bodies of the stoneflies?

Next, copy the color. Scientific study suggests that fish can see in broader spectrums than humans. From a predator perspective, this is not critical. When choosing a fly, try to match the colors you see as closely as you can. If the body of the natural is pale olive and its wings are gray, then a fly that closely matches those features and colors is a practical choice. Remember that water may change the color of an imitation. Oftentimes, the water will darken the colors you see when the imitation is dry.

Then match the size of the natural. It may not be critical that you break out the micrometer, but if a fly is approximately one-half inch long, then an imitation tied on a Size 16 hook will approximate the correct size. Regardless of the hook size, your imitation needs to closely duplicate the size of the natural, giving you predator advantage.

Finally, you should mimic the action of the natural. If it is a mayfly you are imitating, which sits docile on the surface while it is drying its wings, then an imitation that drifts quietly with no drag from the leader or line is the ticket. If you are imitating a caddisfly adult, which flutters and bounces on the surface, then give your imitation some action as it floats through the trout's window.

The same four basic principles apply whether you are trying to imitate a floating adult insect or a subsurface nymph form. The critical variation is that floating flies should float and sinking flies should sink. Sometimes you can observe anglers that have a good imitation but are fishing their flies at the wrong level.

When you follow these principles of imitation, you will beat the odds of selection. The flies that fill your boxes begin to take on specific-use meaning. This does not necessarily mean that you will always be successful, but it sure improves your odds. It is difficult to predict how fish will react in every circumstance. That is both the challenge and the reward of the predator angler.

Psychology of Selection

Now that you have digested all of the selection information, it is time for a brief story about extremes.

I know a gentleman who fishes with just one fly pattern in three sizes—the Royal Coachman. He starts early in the season before runoff and plies the edges of the current with his dry fly. After runoff and all the way through to the fall and into early winter, the Royal Coachman is his only fly. He catches a lot of fish.

Famous angler/writer Ernest G. Schwiebert Jr. carried patterns to match every possible insect and variation of insect stages that he might encounter. He may have had numerous patterns for mayfly species in a variety of shades and sizes. He caught a lot of fish.

These two anglers cover both ends of the selection spectrum. So where does the fly-fishing predator fall on this scale? Should you skew one way or the other? There is not a right answer. Each angler must find his or her own comfort zone.

The key is confidence. One of the most unique characteristics of the psychology of selection is the confidence you have with your choice. When you fish with a favorite pattern that has been successful for you previously and that you have developed a confidence in, you will catch

large margin. Fly tying supports the fly-fishing predator like no other nonfishing undertaking. It provides you with a more intimate understanding of insects and their unique properties. It combines the science of the insect stages with the expression of art and skill. It provides hours of entertainment with improved on-stream results. It is an ideal predator tool.

When you combine the science of biology and entomology with skill, practical knowledge, observation, and experience your predator fly-fishing prowess is enhanced. ∎

more fish with it. You cast it knowing that a fish will take it at any second. You are more attentive to the spot of the cast, to the drift, and to the take. You are ready. You have confidence. When you fish with an imitation that someone else has given you to try, you will focus at first. But if you do not get immediate results, your interest will wane and you confidence will wither. It may be a "hot" pattern for them, but if you do not have confidence, it might not work as well for you.

The fly-fishing predator finds a spot somewhere in the middle of the spectrum. He observes the insects and ties on a favored imitation he has confidence in that resembles the natural he thinks the fish are keying on. He will catch a lot of fish.

The fly-fishing predator, like the great blue heron, mixes experience with instinct when he makes his fly selection. Combine your ability to choose a fly with the skills of casting and reading the water, and the power of the fly-fishing predator will reap great rewards. ■

Chapter Five

Sharpen Your Presentation Strategy

A four-foot, buff-colored bull snake slithers slow and low along a freshly plowed furrow. Every few minutes, he flicks his tongue, trying to pick up the scent of prey. The reptile maintains a flattened profile, tucks his body against the shaded side of the furrow, and holds perfectly still—camouflaged against the mottled background. A dusky field mouse pokes his nose over the lip of the ditch. The snake remains motionless and unnoticed. A mouse can outrun this predator, so the bull snake must be near its prey before striking. The rodent moves within range and the snake strikes.

The same predator instincts that serve the bull snake also serve the fly-fishing predator. Your presentation strategy is the combination of how you approach the fish, your casting position, the cast itself, and the desired drift of the fly. The fly-fishing predator fashions his presentation with a preconceived strategy and does not predicate his results on luck.

It has been said that the angler's ability to deliver a fly properly is more important than the need for the "right" fly. Effective presentation is the more valuable tool. But when you combine a potent presentation strategy with the "right" fly, then you have the fly-fishing predator advantage.

Most fish are opportunistic feeders. That means they are ready and willing to sample a large variety of food types in their diet. Because of this tendency, a fly that has the characteristics of a natural insect—meaning it floats and drifts like a natural insect in a favorable feeding lane—can, and will, produce strikes.

When you compound the knowledge and skill from the previous chapters with a superior presentation strategy, you evolve into a consummate fly-fishing predator.

Effective presentation is a craft that can be honed when you understand and apply the principles of the acronym SUCCESS.

Sneaky

Up-Current

Closer

Confidence

Easier

Seams

Sun-Spots

SUCCESS is the fly-fishing predator's attitude toward presentation.

Sneaky

Your ability to be sneaky is essential to a predator presentation strategy. Like the bull snake, you do not want the prey to perceive your presence until it is too late.

Have you noticed that when you fish with guides or other experienced anglers, they are cautious and quiet? Good anglers cause minimal disturbance in everything they do. Even though most airborne sounds do not penetrate the water, especially when the water is churning through rocky substrate, you do not want to provide the fish any advantage.

This does not mean that you should not speak with your companions or ask them for assistance. It does suggest that there should be less talk. When you converse, use

Bill Frangos sneaks up to a hole to catch a wary trout.

muted tones. Not only does a predator approach his prey silently, but silence allows the complete experience on the river to be more tranquil.

Watch your step. Some anglers look toward the area they intend to fish too much and do not spend enough time looking where they place their feet. Once you are in a proper position for a cast, it is important to focus on your objective. How many times have you or someone you were with stumbled over a boulder or sunken log because it went unnoticed? This commotion is telegraphed through the water, sending an alarm to every fish in the area. The fish become edgy, reducing your odds of success.

It is important to wade with caution. Be attentive to each foot placement. Get a firm grip with one foot before you place the next. Not only does this provide a safer and more stable casting foundation, but fewer fish are disturbed in the process.

The beneficial result of cautious steps and more solid footing is that you will naturally proceed more slowly. Moving at an unhurried pace benefits you in two critical ways. First, you push less water. As you move and water is pushed, it creates ripples on

The author gets low on a meadow stream.

and in the water. These ripples may cause fish to evacuate the area or just go on heightened alert. Either way, your chances of success are reduced. Second, slower movement is harder for the fish to perceive. Fish can see outside the water as well as through the water. They are wary of movement. When you move deliberately, it is much more difficult for fish to discern your presence.

As you walk and wade, a shuffle is the best way to approach your casting position. We have all seen anglers who are powerful waders. With their strength, they can move quickly through the current. A big, powerful stride gets them to their destination faster, but they are likely signaling their arrival on the scene.

Because fish are prey to a variety of animals, they are wary of all movement in their window of observation. This includes both the underwater environment as well as outside the water. Fly-fishing predators must maintain as low a profile as possible. The smaller the stream, the more critical this is because with the shallower depth, the window to the outside environment is greater. Keeping a minimal profile may even involve

Bill Frangos keeps a low profile along the edge of a stream.

crawling along the shore to gain your advantageous position.

A productive angling friend of mine nearly always wades the shoreline bent over to reduce his profile as he moves upstream. He moves assertively and constantly but never seems to create any disturbance. He catches a lot of fish.

Sometimes you must conceal or disguise your cast. The rod waving back and forth is unnatural in this environment and is disturbing to wary fish. False casting must be kept to a minimum, so employ a side-arm cast to avoid the fish's detection.

Inanimate objects such as boulders, trees, and shrubs favor the fly-fishing predator. Use them to hide behind and cast around. It is surprising how close you can get to feeding fish when you conceal yourself behind these obstacles.

A friend and I were once leapfrogging up a small stream. He would get into the stream at a likely spot while I would walk upstream, keeping away from the water for fifty yards before entering the river. This left him undisturbed water to fish. When my partner got up to where I entered, he would get out and move about fifty yards or

The author uses boulders and clothing to match the surrounding area, sneaking up on fish in this boulder section of river.

so above me. After fishing for several hours, we took a break, sitting streamside and chatting. He described a fish that he failed to catch in the last section. The fish was feeding above some deadfall. He had approached the fish from midstream and cast across the current. He said that each time he cast, the fish would stop feeding. When he retrieved his fly and prepared to move, the fish would again begin feeding. He went through this process three times, never putting the fish down, but never catching him, either.

We went back to look over the situation. I suggested he approach the fish's position from below the deadfall and lay a curve cast to the fish. One cast and the fish sipped his dry fly.

When he masked his cast behind the veil of the deadfall, the fish was unaware of this fly-fishing predator's presence.

Look at what you are wearing. Bright, bold colors are easily seen by fish. Those colorful clothes may look good in photographs, but you give fish an advantage when you wear them. Wear muted colors that match the streamside backgrounds. Many anglers have converted to camouflage apparel and accessories that break up their profile and make it increasingly difficult for fish to perceive them. Every advantage you gain increases your effectiveness.

Like the snake that masked his presence in the shadows, you too should be devious. Maximize your predator advantage at every opportunity to sneak up on fish. The closer you can get to the fish, the better you can control your cast and drift.

The better you are at being sneaky, the more fish you will catch.

Up-Current

As mentioned previously, fish in moving water face into the current. They do this for two primary reasons. A fish inhales water through its mouth and presses it across its gill plates as it exhales the water. Life-giving oxygen is extracted in the process. Using the current to accomplish this important action improves efficiency. Trout also depend on the current to provide them with a constant supply of food.

It is also essential to understand that because fish have eyes on the sides of their heads, their view is almost panoramic. As a result, they have less depth perception, but it allows them to detect potential food on both sides as well as above and below their position. From a fly-fishing predator point of view, this is critical to your presentation strategy, because there is a blind spot in the fish's field of view. It lies directly behind the fish.

Before you make your initial cast, observe the direction of flow in the area you intend to fish. Review chapter 3 to predict where you think the fish are holding. This is an important building block in your presentation strategy.

It is also essential that you have a sense of the rate of flow. Rate determines how far above a fish's holding position you should cast your fly. Too far and your fly may be subject to excessive drag; not far enough and you may cause them to stop feeding or scurry away, or you may not provide ample time for the fish to respond.

Fish primarily look forward in anticipation of a moving smorgasbord carried by the current. Depending on the time of year and insect activity, fish may be looking toward the surface to capture flies floating on top or insects suspended in the surface film. They may be watching the mid-water column for immature insects that are emerging from the streambed to the surface. They may be searching downward, trying to detect active, immature insects foraging the rocky substrate. In any case, the goal is to drift your fly imitation from up-current into the fish's area of focus.

Closer

You can get much closer to fish than you imagine if you are deliberate, careful, and crafty. The nearer you can maneuver to a fish, the shorter the cast required to reach him. The shorter your cast, the more control you have. And the more control you have, the more effective you are as a fly-fishing predator.

As mentioned in the previous section, fish have a blind spot directly behind them. Draw on this to improve your advantage. Closer is better.

Review chapter 2 and recall that you have the predator-advantage tools discussed in chapter 1. Your casts are well-controlled when you maximize the advantage of rod length, leader size and length, and your ability to stretch and reach. Just these three elements mean that without extending the fly line from the rod tip, you are already within twenty feet of the fish. It gives you complete control of your cast and drift.

Obstacles in or near the water allow you to approach even closer. This cover enlarges the fish's blind spots. The banks of most of our trout streams have a combination of trees and shrubs, standing logs and deadfall, boulders and rock outcroppings, or high grasses and plants. All of these obstructions provide tremendous cover for the fly-fishing predator. Exploit them.

When the stream is a little off-color rather than clear, you can get even closer. The effect of tinted water is similar to looking through frosted glass windows. One of my favorite times of the year to fish is in early spring, before the complete effect of runoff taints the water. As warmer weather moves in, snow in the upper reaches of the headwaters begins to melt. This causes streams to swell slightly and carry a tinge of color, but not the turbulent muddy water of full-fledged runoff. The trout are hungry, and because of the color distortion, they are less wary. Through that frosted window, we can still make out shapes and movement, but most of the details are distorted.

Getting closer to your prey gives you the predator advantage. You have better control of the situation. Better control means better line management. Better line management reduces drag on the fly. Reduced drag increases your ability to deceive the fish. The better you deceive the fish, the more strikes you get, which improves your SUCCESS.

Confidence

Be assertive when you plan and execute your presentation strategy. Once you have finished this book, you will have all the knowledge to succeed. Your degree of confidence is a direct result of having the ability to cope with every situation.

Your first step in developing more confidence is to imagine that you know the exact location of every fish in the area you are about to approach. This, of course, will not always be true. However, if you follow the principles laid out in chapter 3, you will be correct more often than not.

The author's clothing blends in with the streamside foliage as he works up this cascading stream.

You already know that the personality and character of a stream changes as it follows its course. Each section of river is just a little bit different than the others. This is a part of the appeal of fly-fishing. Complexity is more interesting.

In your mind's eye, etch the image of where you believe the fish are holding. This sets the stage for making your first cast. Too often anglers simply cast to all parts of the stream. This is wasted motion and potentially distracting to the fish.

Position yourself where you have the maximum advantage to cast. Cast with crisp power! Do not allow lazy, inaccurate loops. Power does not mean you should slap the fly down or drive it into the surface of the stream. Crisp power means that you provide enough power in your casting stroke to present your fly to the most opportune spot with maximum efficiency.

While you cast with power, you also need to cast smoothly. An efficient cast is a graceful cast that presents your fly with a minimum of fish-distracting motion.

The most important part about fishing with confidence is the ability to make a quick decision. Observe your surroundings. Evaluate the current and the obstacles. Imagine where you believe the fish to be, set yourself up for your first cast, and then take action with the confidence that you are ready to maximize each opportunity.

The predator tiger sees his prey and is unaffected by distractions. Confident fly-fishing predators are like the tiger in their presentation strategy. They keep their eyes on the target. See where you want your fly to land and proceed with the mechanics to put it there.

Easier

Move yourself to a more desirable position to make your cast easier. The easier the cast, the more productive you become. Remember the basic principle presented in the introduction. Predators live by a common rule. They must capture their prey and expend less energy in the effort than they gain from the bounty. That is the law of survival. The fly-fishing predator is not dependent on catching fish for survival, but he is dependent on catching fish to improve his experience. Taking the easier approach improves efficiency.

In order to put yourself in the most advantageous position, several factors must be considered. The direction of flow determines which direction the fish are facing. The speed of the current dictates how far upstream of the fish you must cast in order to provide the most efficient drift. The depth of the water column affects where the fish may hold and what stage of natural insects they may be eating. Currents, counter currents, and variable currents exert pressure on the line, leader, and fly once they hit the water.

Your improved position before making your cast adds precious additional length of natural, drag-free drift, which enhances your ability to catch more fish.

A critical factor that is often ignored is right behind you. When there are trees, shrubs, cliffs, or rocky outcroppings, it is more challenging to execute an accurate cast. Move to an unobstructed position whenever possible. Sometimes a minimal shift in one direction or another opens up an unobstructed casting avenue.

Obstacles in the stream afford you protection from fish detection. Use these obstacles to get closer more easily.

Seams

Fish lie and feed in seams. Every seam may not be obvious to the casual observer, but fly-fishing predators find them.

Go back and review chapter 3.

As you enhance this skill, more seams become apparent.

Because a seam is created where two different current speeds abut, water flow pauses, and along with it anything floating on or suspended in the water. Seams can be the most productive part of the river.

Another distinctive seam is the line created where two currents come together, even if the currents are of equal speed. A seam of slower water, normally short, is formed right at the inside point of the V where the two flows meet. Fish that hold in these spots have the advantage of food streaming in from both sides. Whenever one stream or branch of a stream meets with another, you can almost always count on fish residing in that seam.

It is common for a side current to be diverted from the main stream by an island for a distance. When this side flow reenters the main stream, it acts just like a tributary, entering the main flow and creating an additional seam.

Your determination to find seams is the tale of two rivers. The trick is finding two rivers disguised as two currents in the midst of a river. Each of the two currents has its own characteristics and can hold fish independently. But the line created where they meet is magical and productive.

One of the reasons fishing pocket water is so productive is that it is a collection of various-sized seams. When you work through pocket water, every seam of slowed current has the potential to hold fish.

The fly-fishing predator is constantly on the lookout for productive seams. If all you did was fish seams all day, you would catch a lot of fish.

Sun-Spots

The position of the sun in relationship to the direction you are fishing is critical in your desire to avoid detection by fish. Avoid bright, sunny areas. Even though the warming rays may feel great on your back, the sunlight illuminates your profile. You are much better off positioning yourself in shadows or filtered light. This reduces the potential of fish recognizing your intrusion.

There is the age-old query, "When is the best time to fish?" Of course, the natural answer is, "Whenever you can!" More often, successful anglers respond with, "Fish early—fish late." When the sun is closer to each horizon, the intensity of the light is reduced. Less light results in a less distinctive outline; therefore, it is much more difficult for the fish to detect their predators. The other advantage of fishing early and late is those times of day are normally when insect activity is most abundant. These insects are also influenced by the intensity of the sun's rays.

As with other parts of this chapter, your presentation strategy is contingent, in part, on the primary direction of streamflow. Be alert to the sun's position and maneuver yourself to less illuminated areas.

The sun's arc varies in its angle at different times of year. In the middle of the summer, when the sun is at its most overhead path in the northern hemisphere, you get

Bill Frangos moves into the shadows to disguise his presence.

primarily east-west shadows. This is considerably different than early spring or late fall, when the sun's arc is farther south and creates more northerly shadows.

Adjust your presentation strategy according to the time of day and time of year to avoid sun-spots. A sun-spot is the part of a river that is illuminated by the sun. Whenever possible, the angler should position himself out of this spotlight.

Shadows are both friends and foes of the fly-fishing predator. Use them to your advantage and eliminate them as a distraction to the fish.

Many of our streams flow through deciduous and evergreen forests. This streamside vegetation casts shaded fields onto the stream's surface that result in areas of filtered light. Filtered sunlight breaks up your silhouette, making it more difficult for the fish to see you.

Use shadows to your advantage. Whenever possible, move your position to where you are camouflaged by the shadows.

Bill Frangos kneels in the filtered light coming through the branches.

The sun's position throughout the season affects your presentation strategy and how you approach each spot. It also affects where the fish hold. I remember fishing a caddis hatch one spring on a large river in Colorado. It was a bluebird day with a bright sun and very few clouds. As the afternoon progressed, the western stream bank cast a narrow band of shaded water that was no more than a foot or two wide. The river was at least fifty feet wide in this section, but all fish activity from about four o'clock to dusk took place in this two-foot swath of dark water. The fish and the ovipositing insects were reacting to the sun's position and were stacked up like cordwood, feeding along the western bank to the near exclusion of the rest of the river.

On the other side of this shadow coin, shadows can be your enemy. Have you ever walked up to a stream while the sun is at your back? There were times when I was not paying attention and I allowed my shadow to fall on the stream surface ahead of me. Trout scurried off in every direction.

All prey use the detection of shadows crossing their view as a sign of a predator lurking nearby. Be more cautious and aware of your shadows to prevent fish from being spooked by your negligence.

Focus on the seven keys of SUCCESS:

Sneaky

Up-Current

Closer

Confidence

Easier

Seams

Sun-Spots

All of these keys are powerful tools to give you predator advantage. But when you combine all of these skills and sharpen your presentation strategy, you will double your SUCCESS!

Chapter Six

Sharpen Your Hooking and Landing Technique

The mottled-gray western screech owl perches on a ponderosa tree limb overlooking a small stream, his yellow eyes keenly looking for movement. Along the bank, near the waterline, he sees a mountain vole moving through tufts of grass. The owl launches from his perch, glides noiselessly toward his prey, and snatches the animal. The bird is careful not to mangle the vole as he flies to his nest. Once there, he parcels out the food to three hungry owlets.

An efficient predator, the owl in brooding season must capture prey and then release them to his young. Like the owl, the fly-fishing predator has broader objectives than the simple catching of prey. He sharpens his skills at catching, landing, and releasing fish to protect a resource.

As you read through this book and develop the skills to become a more efficient predator, you will discover that you catch a lot more fish. But fishing like a predator should not reduce the prey's species. As our human population continues to increase, we put more pressure on our natural resources. Progress, disguised as urban development, reduces the amount of free-flowing water—the habitat of trout. Most accomplished fly-fishing anglers practice catch and release most of the time. This is not to say that many anglers do not appreciate a nice, fresh trout dinner once in a while, but it does mean that we do not need to stock our freezers with the carcasses of dead fish.

Since we are not dependent on catching fish for our major food source, we fish for recreation. Releasing fish unharmed maintains the population for your future fishing excursions as well as for future generations.

The fly-fishing predator, efficient in fooling fish, now has the responsibility to release most of his catch so that the resource is not depleted. This is good stewardship of the stream. In this chapter, the focus is on hooking, landing, and releasing. Too many anglers give little thought to this part of their arsenal. Their primary concentration is on where to fish, what fly to use, and how to get that fly into the proper spot. Those, of course, are important aspects to fly-fishing as well. An effective angler's reward is finding himself attached to a really good fish. At this point, it may be too late to think about landing techniques. The action happens quickly, and if you are just reacting, the fish has the advantage.

Many anglers do an acceptable job of getting fish to take flies. But watch the angler who shouts in frustration over a missed strike. See an angler's shoulders and head hang down like a beaten dog after a long line release—that's when a fish gets off the hook after a brief struggle. Observe the angler who splashes through the shallows, chasing a fish that became unhooked right at the critical moment before the fish is in hand or net. Behold the stymied angler in waist-deep current trying to land a large fish without a net.

The fly-fishing predator plans to release most of the fish he or she catches. However, losing a large fish is a bittersweet experience. There is a special satisfaction in landing, holding, and then releasing one of these beautiful creatures. When we lose one, it is a loss that runs and re-runs through the theater of our minds. We analyze our errors and then try not to repeat them the next time.

The fly-fishing predator is far more successful in this arena because he is attentive to details and reduces or eliminates the ingredients of failure before the first cast.

Hooking

Before you make your first cast, there are three critical components to check.

First, inspect the fly. Make sure the materials used to construct the imitation are bound on the hook properly. Be satisfied with the color, size, and proportions of the fly.

Also look closely at the hook gap to make sure the hook has not inadvertently been bent. A bent hook results in a change in the width of the gap, which might negatively affect its hooking properties. A bend may also create a weak spot in the metal hook.

Second, check the hook point for sharpness. An easy test is to drag the hook across your fingernail. If it bites in, it is sharp enough. If it slides across, it is time to sharpen the point. You can purchase a small hook hone or file to accomplish this. If it has not already been done, this is an ideal time to mash the barb. Many of our stream regulations require that an angler use barbless hooks, but most commercially tied flies have barbs. Use a small pair of needle-nosed pliers to mash the barb flat. A barbless hook will penetrate better; plus, it has the added benefit of being easier to dislodge when releasing fish. This will be covered in greater depth toward the end of this chapter.

Third, inspect the leader, tippet, and knots. Over time, leaders may become brittle. An investment in replacing leaders and tippets regularly will reap you rewards with more fish brought to net. Leaders also become abraded on rocks and branches in the normal course of angling. Each of these nicks and abrasions causes a weak area on the leader. Check it after each fish you land.

Adding a tippet to the end of your leader can add longevity and productivity to your leader. The last few feet of leader get the most abuse. The tippet, which has a consistent diameter of monofilament, takes the brunt of the damage. It is easier and more economical to replace than the leader. Another advantage of the tippet is that as you replace or change flies, you are changing it on a consistent thickness of nylon. If you are tying the fly directly to the leader, every time you change flies, you are working your way up the taper. This means each time you change, the leader gets thicker and stiffer. This affects the way the fly is cast and can be detrimental by causing additional drag.

Finally, when inspecting the leader and the tippet, verify that all of your knots are secure. There are some excellent resources for learning how to tie the knots used in fly-fishing. Learning to tie effective knots adds hours of fishing satisfaction. Weak knots create moments of frustration.

You will hear countless stories about "the big one that got away." A vast majority of these mishaps could have been avoided if the angler had made these three checks. The fly-fishing predator says to himself, "If the next fish I catch is my largest ever, am I ready?"

Mental preparation can be almost as important as hardware and presentation preparation. In chapter 4, I covered the topic of confidence. When you fish with a go-to pattern, you cast knowing that a fish will take it at any second. When this is true, you have prepared yourself mentally to capture the moment as well as the fish.

The fly-fishing predator expects the strike. He maintains a tight connection between the fly and the rod tip. It should not be so tight that it causes drag on the fly but tight enough that there is no slack line that can delay the strike. He is vigilant with his eyes, trying to pick out any movement that might be fish. His muscles are relaxed but ready to react quickly and efficiently.

Expect the strike and catch more fish.

Now that the strike has come when we expect it, it is time to react. Too often, the angler either reacts too slowly or with too much vigor.

The strike for trout should be more of an assertive lift of the rod tip, rather than an aggressive jerk. When you see a fish take the dry fly or you see a movement of the strike indicator, a sharp but short lift of the rod tip is sufficient to set the hook.

I have laughed at my friends or at myself when our strikes were too aggressive. There have been many occasions when a smaller than expected fish takes the fly and then is launched completely out of the water, only to land behind us. The poor, small fish sails through the air disoriented and shaken. When this happens, it is time to lighten up a little.

Timing is a critical element to your success. Unfortunately, timing is not something you can learn from a book. You can read about it. You can imagine it. And you can anticipate it. But the only way to develop effective timing is to practice it . . . on the river . . . catching fish. The good news is that the fly-fishing predator catches more fish on which to practicing his timing.

Hooking more fish is not luck. It is no more luck than reading the water effectively, choosing the right fly, and presenting the fly properly and naturally. When you prepare for the possibilities, you eliminate most of the elements of failure.

Landing

One of the most important things to learn about landing fish is that if a fish is hooked well, even with barbless hooks, you can almost always land it. And if a fish is not hooked well, no matter how carefully you play it, the fish will almost always get away. The key, therefore, is to do things properly to achieve success—set the hook, relax, and enjoy the connection.

Landing a fish is broken down into three sequential parts—the initial hooking and the first few seconds that follow, playing the fish to gain control, and landing the fish gently so as not to harm it.

When you hook a fish, what you do in the first few seconds makes all the difference in the world.

If there are no obstructions in the immediate area, the most effective strategy is to let the fish have its way. Let it do what it wants. You want it to expend energy so that you can maintain control. After the fish exhibits it initial flurry of activity, it will settle down somewhat and be easier to land.

If you hook a fish near logjams, ledges, downfall, undercut banks, or boulders, matters may get more complicated. When you hook a fish near hazards, apply side pressure away from the danger. You can exert little pressure straight up, but you can apply substantial pressure when you keep your rod tip close to the surface.

Most fish when first hooked will run, jump, or hide. When they run, the power they have is exhilarating. When they jump, you get the thrill of both the surge and the visual stimulus of these magnificent creatures taking to the air—outside their natural environment. When they want to hide, the angler has additional challenges.

In these first few seconds, you want to avoid letting the fish get below you. This is the single biggest problem the angler faces, especially with larger fish.

In this next section, you will learn how to sharpen your skills at playing fish under a variety of circumstances. It is impossible to explore every situation. You will be faced with multiple variations, but the basics will serve you well.

The amount of time you play a fish is dependent on the size of the stream and the size of the fish. You must be sensitive to the fact that you want to play a fish long enough to tire him out, but not too long, which may fatigue the fish past its ability to recuperate. When you horse a fish in without tiring it, landing is more difficult and its thrashing and flopping around may cause external and internal injuries. Playing a fish too long causes lactic buildup, which may cause irreparable internal damage.

As mentioned, fish will run, jump, or hide. How you handle each situation will dictate your success at landing each fish.

Fortunately, most fish when hooked, especially when you are presenting your fly up current, will run upstream or to one side or the other. This is one of the easiest circumstances to deal with. You should apply light pressure to the fish as it struggles. Light pressure allows the fish to keep its head facing into the current. It then must fight both your pressure and the current, which wears the fish down. When a fish can keep its head facing into the current, it remains calmer than if you exert more pressure and try to turn it.

Depending on the size of the fish, the fight should last only a few minutes. The fish will give up the major struggle and then you can bring it gently back down with the current to your position for landing and releasing.

When fish jump and give you an aerial display, it is stimulating. It is fun for you and energy-draining for the fish. Most trout only make a few jumps, so enjoy them while you can. There is a concern with larger fish that when the fish jumps, it can land on the leader and break the delicate tippet. Your best strategy when this happens is to lower the rod tip slightly, which reduces some of the tension on the line. This lessens the risk of the leader breaking. After a few leaps, the fish is normally subdued quickly and can be brought to your landing position.

It is not unusual for a fish to dive to the bottom of the stream when hooked. Anglers suspect that hiding toward the bottom or under obstructions provides fish with a sense of confidence that they can escape predation. When a fish hunkers down and gives you a tug-of-war, it is a great sensation. When they do this, the best technique is to give the fish a little side pressure. If you pull straight up, you cannot exert as much leverage, which gives the fish some advantage. Side pressure moves the fish and makes them work against the current as well as the tension from the rod.

When they take refuge under a boulder, logjam, or undercut bank, the risk of losing the fish is higher. In most circumstances, the angle of your leader is your best indicator of what to do next. As the fish drives into its protective sanctuary, the line follows his line of entry. Your best course of action is to try to get the fish to come out the same way he went in. The angle of the leader provides the angle to exert pressure. When a fish becomes entangled in underwater snags, you have to try your best to get him untangled and hope he remains hooked. There is no magic solution to this situation. Sometimes you win and sometimes the fish wins. Either way, it is stimulating.

The most challenging situation is when a fish runs downstream straight toward you. This behavior creates a variety of problems. Normally, you cannot strip or reel line fast enough to keep up with this rush. As a result, this takes tension off the hook and presents an opportunity for the fish to throw the hook and swim away. If the hook holds, the slack line still can snag on bottom structure. If the line lodges tight enough, all shock-absorbing properties are eliminated and there is a high risk of the leader snapping and the fish continuing its bolt downstream. If you are still hooked up after those two potential mishaps, you still have a major threat facing you. When a fish passes you and continues downstream, it now has most of the advantage. Now, instead of the current working against him, it is working for him and against you. Even if you manage to stop the run and turn the fish, it is very difficult to retrieve line from a fish downstream from your position.

The best technique is to follow the fish and try to get to a position below or downstream from the fish. If you cannot get below the fish because of obstructions, you still have some hope.

Once the fish has turned back and faces into the current, try to let an additional ten to twenty feet of line out. The theory is that the extra line will belly below the fish to create downstream pressure from the current on the fly line. When the fish feels this pressure, it will cause him to swim away from it and move back upstream. This has not always worked for me, but it is worth a try when you are in this predicament.

Now that you have fought the good fight and have moved the fish into a position where you are likely to capture him, there are three basic ways to accomplish the feat.

The first and the easiest is to carry a landing net. Since the fly-fishing predator is

The author has hooked and let the fish have his way for a while.

primarily a catch-and-release angler, you want to capture the fish as gently and carefully as possible to ensure the fish's recovery when you release him back into his environment. There are some wonderful catch-and-release nets with soft mesh that do not abrade the fish's body.

When you have a fish in position—tight, short line, rod held high, fish with its head up and gliding toward you—simply dip the net in the path of the fish, slide the fish into the mesh, and lift him from the water. Once the fish is in the net, you should release tension on the line and dip the net back into the water slightly while you prepare for the release. This will keep the fish moist and allow the fish's gills to continue to breathe rather than suffocate.

There are three DON'Ts when landing a fish with a net.

- Don't stab at the fish when you get him close. This will just spook him, creating panic and jeopardizing your success ratio.

The fish is now being pulled toward the author in preparation for landing.

- Don't try to come down on a fish with the net from out of the water. Your chances at landing the fish are slim and high on unintentionally releasing him.

- Don't chase the fish around with the net. Besides creating chaos and panic in the fish, this will also reduce your chance of success. If you do not get him gently in the net the first time, regroup and try again with the proper technique.

The second effective way to land a fish is to gently slide him onto a soft shoreline. If you are in a position to bring the fish to you, a soft, sandy, or grassy bank is your best choice. The characteristic of a stream along this type of shore is that it gradually changes from deep water to shallow water to shoreline. The shallower water takes the leverage away from the fish. He cannot create any power when he is out of the water.

Once you have tired the fish somewhat, exert side pressure toward the shore you are standing on. As the water gets shallower, the fish will fall onto one side and slip into a position for you to unhook and release him.

The author dips the net into the water and slides the fish over it.

There are three DON'Ts for this technique.

- Don't drag a fish up onto the shore until some of the fight is out of him. If the fish is still flopping around, there is a good chance the fish will injure himself.

- Don't bring a fish up onto a rocky shoreline. Rocks can be abrasive on his skin and the hard, sharp edges can be lethal.

- Don't drag the fish all the way up the shore and onto dry land. Keep the fish in the shallows so that his skin does not dry or get rubbed off.

The final technique for landing a fish is useful when you are wading without a net and getting to a shore is difficult or impossible.

When you find yourself in this situation, there is a fairly simple solution. Once you have played the fish for a period of time and most of the fight is out of him, you can gently coax him to your side. If you are right-handed, this will be to your left side and to your right if you are left-handed. Reel up any slack line and, with very little fly line out of the tip of your rod, slide the fish next to your leg. Right-handed anglers can pin the fish with their left hand (and vice versa). This is much easier than trying to grab a swimming fish. This puts you in an ideal position to remove the hook and release the fish.

There are three DON'Ts for this technique.

- Don't grab the leader in your attempt to control the fish. Once you grab the leader, any shock-absorbing properties of the line and the rod are eliminated. There is a good chance the fish will break off.

- Don't try to pin the fish until he is sufficiently fatigued. A fish that still has his fight can create comedic gyrations when you try to land him this way.

- Don't try this technique if you are in water that is more than three feet deep. If the water is lapping at the top of your chest waders, you should move into shallower water or be carrying a net.

All of these techniques require that you wear the fish down . . . not out. You do not want to overtax the fish's system. When you release the fish, he should be able to recover without complications.

Even if you execute good hooking, fighting, and landing skills, you might not always get the results you want. I recently returned from a fishing trip in Alaska. We were pursuing monstrous rainbows on the Kenai River. At one point, I had hooked, played, fought, and brought in a twenty-eight-inch, heavy-bodied rainbow to the side of the boat. Just as we were preparing to net the giant, he got spooked. He had one more spurt, took a dive around the anchor line, and was off. For me, this would have been the trout of a lifetime. We would have released him anyway, but, alas, I sure wanted the photo. At that point, about all you can do is wish the fish well and vow to return another day for another shot at him.

Landing fish is unpredictable. Examine each situation and prepare for the unexpected. Be flexible in your techniques and land more fish.

Releasing

As mentioned previously, the fly-fishing predator catches a lot of fish. Most of them should be released back into the stream to maintain a renewable resource.

There are several factors that will make releasing fish easier on you and the fish.

Use barbless hooks. If you follow the hooking and landing guidelines and keep

This brown trout is gaining his strength in the shallows so he can swim back to freedom.

tension on the fish, the hook should not come out. Once the fish is landed, the hook backs out easily. This is quicker for you and less stressful on the fish.

In most situations, it is advisable to not remove the fish from the water. All of the landing techniques I have given you allow you to release the fish without ever lifting the fish from the water. Remember, fish breathe by extracting oxygen from water. Any time fish are removed from the water, they gasp for oxygen, which they cannot get from the air. If you want to photograph a fish, position yourself for the shot. Just before the camera click, lift the fish to the position in the shot and then quickly resubmerge the fish.

Before handling fish for hook removal or photos, it is advisable to wet both hands. The slimy surface of fish is for their protection. Your dry hands may break that protection and allow fungus to colonize. This simple infraction can be lethal to fish.

Many anglers have adopted a quick release tool that slides down the leader, unhooks the fly with a gentle twist, and releases fish without ever touching them. This is the least invasive way to release when done properly.

Facing page, top:
The author lifts the fish
from the water for the photo.

Facing page, bottom:
The nice rainbow is
revived and released
gently back to the river.

Right: Bill Frangos
hefts a nice fish for a
memorable photo.

Below:
Bill cradles the fish under
his belly and holds the
fish upright by the tail. In
a few moments, the fish
quickly swims away.

If you need to handle a fish, you may want to turn the fish upside down, which normally reduces squirminess. This will make the process easier and quicker.

After you have removed the hook, gently submerge the fish back into the stream. Cradle the belly of the fish with one hand and lightly hold the fish just in front of the tail with the other. You can control the fish while he works his gills, collecting rejuvenating oxygen. When you see the gill plates pulsating steadily and the fish can hold its upright posture, release the fish with a gentle push back into quiet water. When the fish is ready, he will move to a safer position, again hidden from his predators.

One of the key benefits of becoming a fly-fishing predator is the simple fact that you will catch more fish. This increase in productivity carries with it a responsibility to protect the fish you are catching. Hooking, landing, and releasing fish properly assures you that the next time you fish that section of river, there will be prey waiting for your predator skills.

CHAPTER SEVEN

Predator

Fly-Fishermen

Reap the Rewards

Bill pulled his SUV into my driveway, still shrouded in the early morning darkness. On the horizon, a sliver of light outlined the mountain range that rises east of Albuquerque After loading my fishing gear in the back of the vehicle, I topped off my travel mug with steaming coffee and hopped into the passenger seat.

We exchanged our normal inquiries about families and work and then got down to more serious discussions about fishing, fly tying, gear, and the latest jokes.

 The first thing a predator does when he is hungry is go hunting. The predator begins his search in the most successful hunting grounds from his past experiences. He recognizes the areas that have produced nourishment before. He prowls likely areas based on practicality.

Bill headed the car toward a watershed that has several streams we fished successfully together over the years. We would have several choices once we reached a specific road juncture. This was to be a single-day trip, so we did not plan to explore new waters. We stayed with the tried and trusted.

Gear being prepared and organized for the day's adventure.

After discussing our options, we settled on a canyon section of stream that veers away from the road for a couple of miles. This section gets less fishing pressure than most of the stream because of its limited accessibility. Not only that, but we had caught and released many fish on previous trips, so we anticipated a productive day.

The weather cooperated. Fluffy, white clouds promised intermittent sun and shade. We liked it this way because the sun would warm the air without warming the water too quickly, a combination good for us as well as the fish.

 The predator works a hunting area from the perimeter first. His nostrils flare and his eyes search for signs of other predators. He wants to hunt without interference. He must sneak up on his prey to be rewarded.

As we pulled into the parking area, we were delighted to not see any other vehicles. Like a lot of other things in life, being first is best. Being first on a small stream gives you an advantage. The fish have not seen another angler for a while and are therefore less wary.

Routine is an important part of the predator fly-fisherman's strategy. As we set up our fishing gear, we tend to follow patterns. Fishing equipment comes out first and gets assembled. We check to make sure we have the right fly boxes for the expected insect activity. We inspect our leaders and tippet material. We verify that our vests are stocked with what we deem to be the necessary tools of the trade.

Next we don our waders, pack our lunches in our vests, and slip on our vests. We mentally go through our checklists, lock up the vehicle, and set off for the river.

The predator hunts by necessity. He stands stationary in the shadows, waiting and watching. He must be diligent in his search. He must not rush. He is pure business.

We always appreciate the opportunity to get out, spend some time together doing what we love, and smile to each other in anticipation of catching and releasing a few fish. We breathe in the fresh mountain air as even broader grins work their way across both of our faces.

On this particular day, we walked a short distance up the river to distance ourselves from where most anglers start. The investment in a ten-minute walk usually provides immediate and increased results. As we worked our way upstream, we observed a few early-morning caddisflies fluttering in and out of the streamside shrubs.

The predator reaches a clearing with a small stream flowing along its border. He crouches in the shadows of bushes to hide in the shadows so that the unsuspecting prey will not detect his presence. He waits. Not a muscle is moving, but he is ready to take advantage when opportunity presents itself.

We picked an open spot to string up our rods, stretch and straighten our lines and leaders, select our starting fly patterns, and determine which side of the stream each of us would fish.

We often fish this way. Even though this stream is small and a single angler could easily cover it all, we like the social aspects of fishing side by side. Along any given section, sometimes Bill will have the better water and at other times I will. Either way, we both like seeing the other guy fish with success almost as much as having success ourselves. Well, almost!

On this day, Bill went right, I went left. The left is a little easier because we are both right-handed. We both knew we would switch later in the day.

Bill started with a two-fly combination composed of an elk hair caddis dry fly with a small Copper John nymph as a dropper. I decided to fish just a single foam-bodied caddis dry. We had not seen a fish feeding on the surface, but I had high hopes.

Bill moved into position while I applied dry fly floatant to my caddis. The current was primarily on his side of the river at this spot. He began plying a nice, deep run between two in-stream boulders. The current pinched between these rocks and then fanned out with a seam on either side.

I watched as he cast his flies above the rocks, kept his rod high and followed the drift with his rod tip. After a couple of casts and drifts through the gap, a feisty little brown trout grabbed the dropper, which sank the dry fly. Bill sharply lifted the rod tip and stuck the fish. After a short but lively fight, the small fish came to hand and was carefully released. It was a good start to the day.

He ran a couple more floats around both sides of the boulders but got no more action. It was my turn to perform. Above where we stood, most of the water pushed against a grassy bank on my side. The hole was deep, which slowed the flow and created a nicely defined current line revealed by a narrow line of foam that hugged the left bank. Overhanging grasses trailed in the current, suggesting an undercut bank and a very fishy spot.

I moved upstream and started in the lower part of the hole. I dropped my dry fly alternately between spots a few inches from the bank and those about a foot out from the grasses, occasionally venturing a little farther out. I was prospecting to find out where the fish might be holding this early in the morning. Dewdrops hung on blades of grass and the morning sun had not yet found this part of the stream.

This little run was only about thirty feet long from head to tail, so it did not take long for me to work my way through it. I got no action in the lower part and I was beginning to wonder if I needed to add a dropper until things heated up on the surface.

I reached the upper part of the run where the primary current tumbled off a rock ledge and collided with the left bank. The water bulged at this spot and then turned downstream to form the run. I did not get a fish to come up in the spots I expected, and Bill shook his head because the run looked so promising.

There was a small patch of flat water about one foot in diameter just above where the current ran into the bank. I climbed onto the bank and crawled into a position to make the cast while staying out of the fish's window. I cast my caddis to the spot, kept my rod high, and let the fly float for a moment with no leader or line on the surface to cause drag.

The fly sat there with nearly no movement. In a flash, the fly disappeared in a splashy rise. A nice brown trout bolted into the run and then held in the current below me. I kept my rod high with tension on the fish and worked my way back down the streambank to a position just below the fish. After a few more minutes, I applied a little side pressure and slid the fish up onto the soft, grassy bank. We admired the soft, yellow fish and I released him gently back into the current. He held his position, finning to keep himself upright while pumping water through his gills. After a moment, he sank and drifted under the bank to regain his strength to feed and fight again.

The morning continued on a similar pattern. Sometimes Bill caught a few fish and I would not see any. Sometimes I picked up fish and Bill did not. The stream changed character every couple hundred feet, which is normal for this kind of freestone mountain stream. Sometimes the water would flow over boulders, creating ideal pocket water we could fish from both sides, picking fish from the pockets as we continued upstream. Sometimes the bottom of the canyon would flatten and we would have a section of meadow-type fishing where the stream created S-curves. We would prowl the banks without wading and ply the undercut banks for hiding fish. Sometimes the current gouged a deep trough right down the middle and we would work both of the edges between the faster current and the flat water shallows. Where there was a drop off from the shallows to the deeper section, we picked up a few fish.

In each of these changing personalities of the river, our presentation and approach to the fishing varied a little, but neither of us changed flies except for one nasty incident when a spruce tree reached out and robbed me of my fly. We both picked up fish regularly, but neither of us felt the fish were feeding aggressively.

A predator puts himself into a position to be successful. As the terrain changes, the predator moves to a new position to gain advantage over prey.

We approached a bend in the river bordered by a logjam on the right-hand side. It would have been nearly impossible for Bill to fish from his side, so he waded across to my side and joined me. We decided to alternate fish through this run and then break for lunch.

I had the honors, so I cast my fly along the edges of the tangled wood where the current slipped out from beneath the jam. One of the biggest fish we had seen so far slipped out from beneath the protective cover and inhaled my dry fly. I immediately put down stream pressure on him with my rod in an attempt to accomplish two important things. First, in order to fight and then land the fish, I had to clear him away from the dangerous sticks hanging in the water. Second, if I could move the fish and the disturbance of the fight downstream, then the commotion would not put down the rest of the fish in the hole.

The trout was not a jumper, and the quick pressure caught him off guard, so our tug-of-war was staged below the hazardous stack of logs and sticks. Bill cheered and took a few photos as I netted the fish to protect him from beating himself up on the rocky shore.

A very nice fourteen-inch brown—big for this stream—was revived in the current and tenderly released into the hole below us.

Bill was up next, and on the first cast he was rewarded with a strike on his nymph, and a small fish easily came to his hand.

I moved upstream, and while attempting a curved cast round a hanging log, I promptly snagged my hook into a log as I tried to cast my fly into a tight spot. This happens occasionally. It is part the game. If I am not trying to get into tight spots where I know fish are lurking, then I will not get hung up. It is a risk/reward kind of thing. I take the risk, because when it works I am often rewarded with the best fish of the day.

By this time, we had worked our way to the head of the hole. I let my line out and moved downstream to clear space for Bill to fish the area where I fouled. He made several casts into the current and let the flow carry his flies to the front end of the jam. On his fourth cast, just as the fly reached the edge of the logs, a fish sipped his dry fly from the surface. He swung his rod to the left as he struck the fish. The trout held his ground and did not budge from his spot under the logs. It was a standoff for a short time as each of them tried to exert his will. Bill was smiling, and if the fish could, I am sure he would have been frowning.

Eventually, the fish showed signs of fatigue and his position slipped a little downstream and out from the snags by a few yards. Bill continued to apply force to the left. Slowly, the fish eased from under the tangle and away from the danger. Bill gingerly netted the fish, posed for a few photos and released the twin of the fish I had previously landed.

After this battle was over, I waded into the run and retrieved my fly. It was a grand way to finish the morning, which left us in high spirits and with positive expectations for the afternoon.

After a kill, the predator takes a break. Energy is stored, and then when conditions again become favorable, he goes back to the hunt.

While eating lunch in a shady clearing we reminisced about fish caught and fish lost. We discussed the health of the river and the vivacity of the fish. We were curious about the lack of insect activity. We speculated that with the partly cloudy skies, the water temperature had not warmed sufficiently to get the bugs moving. Most of the cloud cover had drifted east and it appeared that we would have a mostly clear afternoon.

We hoped that if the water warmed some mayflies would emerge and that the fish would hungrily look up. We also expected that the caddisflies that had been resting in the bushes earlier would move to the stream for ovipositing, which should also trigger fish to feed on the surface.

As we finished lunch and prepared to get back in the water, Bill noticed a few small, gray mayflies gracefully flying from the stream to the nearby bushes. We looked upstream to the next hole, which had a center-stream plunge pool with flat water on either side. Below the main current was a deep, slow run as a tail-out. Fish were

Releasing a nice brown trout.

dimpling the water in the tail-out, and as we expected, they had begun to key on the emerging mayflies.

Bill put on a gray comparadun with a trailing emerging nymph as a dropper. I choose an Adams dry fly. I took the right side of the stream this time, and Bill worked the left. Bill was first to get into a fish when a brown trout took the trailing fly. I soon matched him with a lively, jumping trout of my own.

For about an hour, the action was fast and furious for both of us. Every time we found flat water at the tail of faster current, the fish were feeding on the hatching mayflies. Then, just a quickly as the fish had turned on to the hatch, they stopped.

We fished the next several holes but went fishless. A smattering of clouds rolled in and put us under the shade. We stopped and chatted about what our next strategy should be.

We watched a few caddis moving along the streamside, with an occasional fly dipping and bouncing off the surface. The females were dropping their eggs into the water. This was a good sign. We expected that in the next half hour or so, the activity would increase and the fish would notice.

Since nothing was happening with the mayfly imitations we were using, we both shifted to elk hair caddis dries. There were only about two hours of light left, so we felt it was the ideal time for caddis action.

We plied the edges behind every rock and boulder, the slicks downstream from obstructions, the runs, the riffles, and the eddies. Unfortunately, we only caught a few fish. We were beginning to get discouraged when the cloud cover broke and evening sunshine peaked through and lit up the stream again.

Almost immediately, the fishing turned on. Whenever we plopped a fly onto a likely holding spot, a fish would make a slashing rise. The fish we were catching were not large, but we sure were catching a lot of them.

As the light waned, it got more difficult for us to see our flies, but the fish seemed to have no problem. We continued to catch fish when they hooked themselves. We laughed, because even without the benefit of the normal visual clues, the fish were entertaining us.

 Once prey becomes more difficult to catch, the predator moves to a resting place to preserve energy and wait for the next opportunity.

Finally, we reeled in our flies and called it a day. We saluted the river and the fish. We thanked our lucky stars for the tremendous day on the river and a successful day of fishing.

We bushwhacked our way back along the streamside, remembering and commenting on certain fish from distinctive holes we passed on our way back to the car. The dim light allowed us to see pretty well, but we both stubbed our toes on unseen rocks and laughed as we avoided falling on our faces.

After stowing our gear while enjoying cold, refreshing beverages, we sat on the tailgate and enjoyed the encroaching nighttime sights and sounds as the sky became ever darker.

Driving home, we reveled over the variety of fishing opportunities we had experienced. The circumstances changed repeatedly, and we had to change which flies we used as well as our tactics to match what was going on with the fish and the insects. It made for a challenging but interesting day. We were rewarded with success as we solved each of the riddles.

Predator fly-fishing is about the challenge—the personality of the stream on that day and time, the environment, the weather, the friends, the fish, and the results. No two days are ever alike, and that is what makes it so interesting and rewarding.

As Bill pulled up to my house, we discussed plans for the next trip. We always find anticipation a powerful stimulus. ■

Postscript

Enjoy the Journey

The immature hawk sits on a fence post. His ruffled feathers have not yet revealed the markings of an adult red-tail. He notices movement at the base of a sagebrush near a ridge. He lifts into the air on powerful wings. As he nears his prey, his telltale shadow sweeps the ground in front of him. A rabbit ducks into the base of the brush and the young bird veers off.

A fox kit sneaks along the shadow of a tall spruce. He mimics his mother, listening for potential prey scratching for food in the pine needles matted under the tree. His ears cock at the sound coming from the opposite edge of the shadows. A small field mouse is scavenging for seeds. The young fox turns his head. The mouse sees the movement and scurries into his hole.

The young, spotted bobcat lifts her nose to the breeze. Varied scents waft through the air. One of the odors catches her attention, and she notices a chipmunk sitting on a boulder preening itself. She begins a careful stalk in the rodent's direction. Because of her carelessness, she snaps a twig, alerting the chipmunk. He dives down into a crack between the rocks, avoiding the cat's leap.

None of us start with immediate success.

Becoming a fly-fishing predator is a journey of learning. And, like any long journey, it begins the same way—with the first step; and those first efforts are often rudimentary and clumsy.

Our early casting efforts are ungainly. We create bird's nests of tangles with every other cast. We cannot seem to master either direction or distance. When we do manage to make a cast that is on line, the fly slaps on the water and every fish in the hole bolts into hiding.

We approach the stream and cast into many different spots, hoping for the best. Some of the water is so shallow that the only thing our fly is floating over is the bare gravel bottom. Some of the casts go into flat water with no current, and the only thing that sees our fly is the mosquito larvae hanging in the surface film. Some of our casts land in the center of the current and are quickly washed down around our legs before we can begin stripping line.

A few of our days on the river without our mentors are curious. We fish the fly we used last time that gave him success. There are flies swarming along the stream, but the fly at the end of the leader drifts unmolested.

As we approach each part of the river, we are at a quandary as to where or how to put the fly into a position to give us the best shot at catching fish. Overhanging tree branches get in our way. Tree limbs grab the fly on our back casts. In-stream obstructions create all kinds of problems.

But through it all, in spite of our clumsy efforts, sometimes we catch fish. We are thrilled with the fight and appreciate the beauty of this wild and wily creature. The fish flops at our feet, and we unceremoniously try to grab the squirming trout. In the ensuing chaos, the fish flips off the hook and swims frantically back into the protection of the stream's depths.

We have all been there.

In this book, I have tried to put the required predatory skills into a logical order. However, when you are on the river, the logical order may or may not exist.

One of the allures of the fly-fishing adventure is the interconnected complexity of the land, water, fish, and you. Every time you fish, the formula of the experience will be a little different. Even if you fish the same water over and over again, you will never have the same day twice.

Each opportunity to fish is a learning experience. Every time you learn something new, you add to your physical and emotional satisfaction.

In some small way, I hope I have added something to that learning experience. Even though I consider myself a fly-fishing predator, I learn something every day on the river about the water, about the insects, about the fish, and about myself.

I have read hundreds of accounts on why we fly-fish. Most of them capture a part of the reason for me. Not one of them captures every part of what goes on in my mind. I suspect they never will. That is because the reasons for me are mixed and personal. Those other writers have never lived or fished in my shoes and have never had my experiences. So, too, I can never live or fish in your shoes or know your experiences.

We fish because we can and because we enjoy it.

Enjoy the journey.

It is worth every step! ■